MW01632569

Don't Be Invisible Be Fabulous
Volume 7

It's Okay To Value Me

Compiled by

Dorris Burch

Don't Be Invisible Be Fabulous, Volume 7:
It's Okay To Value Me

Published by Fab Factor Publishing
Tinley Park, IL
www.thefabfactor.com

ISBN: 978-0-578-31466-2

Cover design, layout, and typesetting:
Fab Factor Publishing

Cover photo: Charles Taitt

This book is for every woman to remember…

Don't Be Invisible. Be Fabulous!

CONTENTS

The Fabulous Dorris Burch

INTRODUCTION

A lot of women ask, "When is it OK to share my private stuff publicly?" *But what if people think x y z? Or it's too vulnerable? Or it's too raw?* I want to tell you this: it is these doubts and fears that propel the shame that so many women are prisoners too. Secrets kill. Stories heal.

My guiding principle continues to be asking, "could this be of value to my community?" Could the sharing of this story, this insight, this pain, serve as a way to connect, teach, grant permission, or bring in a little more humor or joy to my readers. I know that it can be hard to determine how much to write, or what to write, or what details to share, or not share, but it's important to keep coming back to what could be of value to my readers. When you can tie your writing to being useful in some way, I find the best stories emerge, for great storytelling is vulnerability with a lesson.

I don't love talking about the weather, the latest pop culture news or surface level stuff. I love to dive deep into the extra-ordinary, the emotions, the true feelings. The biggest breakthrough I've had in my life is that I AM NOT ONE THING. Try it. It's a gamechanger. I not only discovered this new idea that I'm not one thing—I actually gave myself permission to embody it. And I say to you today, that you have permission to be more than one thing. You even have permission to be seemingly opposite things. You have permission to give voice to ALL parts of you. And you soooooooo have permission to bring that into your brand, your biz, and your badassery. In fact, I dare you to do so. It gives you visibility. It gives you depth. But most of all, it gives you freedom.

I remember the day I sat down to forgive myself. Candle lit. Journal open. Phone off. This was sacred. It had to be. If I truly wanted to heal. And I did. Want healing. The pain in my soul had cried out for it. So, I sat and wrote a letter to myself from the most gentle, loving, mother voice I could find. And what transpired was a day of full-out, fired-up… crying.

> I cried for all the times I thought I didn't deserve to use my voice.
>
> I cried for all the times I didn't believe in myself.
>
> I cried for all the times I chose to be kind instead of empowered.
>
> I cried for all the times I gave a piece of my soul in exchange for playing small in my business.
>
> I cried to release the…. fear.

I had to share these thoughts with you about forgiveness, because it is such an important topic. This has come up for me as I create new levels of success and step out to be even more seen.

As you know if you wanna share your light with the world and create real change, you always have to start with yourself. And the work is never done, right? New levels of expansion are always waiting!

There are periods when I'm so busy that I work more on my FabFirmations and my soul goals than I do on the deeper healing. But when I'm in the middle of a real up-level, even if I'm busy, my soul won't let me gloss over the important stuff. That's when the real inner work and healing takes place. That's why I love being an entrepreneur, because at the core it's really about a spiritual journey full of expansion.

I am in the middle of a new frequency upgrade now and this expansion is so deep, so part of my truth, that I have been called to dive back into my interior and keep exploring. I thought there was an area where the work was done. I thought I had forgiven myself. Let me explain… years ago I manifested lack as a symbol of my shame around my worth, and my money (and yes, they were all interconnected). I had so much shame around my money and my worth as a woman entrepreneur and I needed to forgive myself. Yes—the real truth that I had been avoiding was—I needed to forgive me. I created my own healing ritual and the day I forgave myself was the day that I knew I would have a Billion Dollar Empire. That was years ago.

Now, today I take a deeper look. As I take a stand for my worth and in doing so, really take a stand for <u>all</u>

women's worth, I take a deeper look. And what I see is this... yes, I have forgiven, but there are still pieces left over that I must watch and make sure don't get outta hand. As a recovering Corporate Good Girl, I can be super hard on myself and if I don't practice self-care, being super hard on myself can turn into judgment, which can turn into faulting, which can turn into shame, which can turn into playing small. Luckily the badass Fabulous Woman in me, doesn't let the Corporate Good Girl go too far. I am doing the work and forgiving myself as many times as needed. And what I notice now is there are still areas where I judge myself too harshly. I notice that I must practice more compassion, more self-care, more radical appreciation. I notice (as we teach in Voice & Visibility Program) that I am not one thing. I am shadow and light. I am all. I am everything. And that is beautiful and OK and not to be judged. I notice and I deepen into my truth. I notice and I love. And as I do this, I am willing to shine brighter. I am willing to take a stand for my gifts. I am willing to be seen. I am willing to receive wealth and abundance as I serve.

I share this because I want to remind you to be kind and forgiving towards yourself. If you are a leader, or a visionary, or a healer, or a heart-centered woman (which I know you are if you're part of my tribe) then you must do this work. You must do this work if you're stepping out and being seen. You must do this work if you want to receive more wealth. You must do this work, because you are a beacon of light, and in order to stand tall in your message you have to be clean and clear on the inside. The energy you come from must be grounded and intentional and then you are able to receive—the business, the love, the money, the success—it all starts with our energy.

Because you are a sensitive soul and sensitive souls often leave their criticism for themselves, here's my invite to you...

- Dig deep into your truth and see where you are still judging, shaming, and faulting.
- Notice how that judgment/shame/faulting feels in your body
- And then breathe into that place and say "I forgive myself" over and over and over... until your body really hears it.

The power of a woman's voice, loud and clear, coming deep from her truth, sharing her message... is undeniable (and sexy).

As I read each chapter for this book. These chapters are filled with depth, emotion, rawness and realness. These women wanted more & they knew they were worth more.

They've experienced the highs and lows of life, the rollercoaster ride, and they've found practices and fundamental truths that brought them back to themselves.

For anyone out there that feels like they are a walking shell of who they truly are, you are NOT ALONE. This book invites us all to uncover who we truly are and most importantly to value ourselves.

If you're in tune, you might be releasing the old (and that can get... emotional) as you open to the new. And so we make emotions wrong. We resist it. We try to ignore it.

So let me tell you... there's no way out, but through.

And sometimes the deep dark pit is necessary for your heroine's journey. Know that your emotions have a message… it has a purpose… and it needs to move so you can release it. When tapping into BIG desire and purpose, you will be taken to the depths of your Being and you will meet up with all that you've tried to hide. You will reconnect with long lost wounds. And your fears will be more than happy to say, "Hello." This. Is. Normal. It means you are about to break through to a new level. If you move through it. No ignoring or resisting allowed! You will learn from it. And the fabulous part? If you dare to dive into the emotion and explore the energies within you will make friends with the dark. You will see that it is part of the light. You will learn to honor your ability to deeply feel. Supporting all these women claim their voice was AMAZING.

Today I ask you... what is your voice longing to express and share? What journey will you take your community on? Most importantly say to yourself … It's Okay To Value Me.

Remember –

Don't Be Invisible. Be Fabulous!

The Fabulous Dorris Burch

Wendy Babcock

THE CALM AFTER THE STORM

Sudden shock rolled through me like an ocean wave during a storm. I felt as though I was watching as the dark clouds billowed above come right at me. While I knew exactly what to expect, as soon as it actually hit me – it rolled my emotions like a barrel in the depths of the water and waves. The storm was just starting.

Not recognizing your own body in the mirror is something that can only be experienced and not really explained. For months I prepared for this moment. I read about it, joined groups on social media that discussed it and I felt totally prepared. Yet somehow standing there in my full-length mirror with nothing but five drains hanging from my hips and under my arms sent me into a full meltdown.

This was the day I came home from my bilateral prophylactic mastectomy with DIEP flap reconstruction.

Let me take you back to October 2015. I was 40 years old and having my very first mammogram. I worked at the hospital where the exam was being performed so it was a little awkward having my co-worker handle my breasts as if we were merely shaking hands. Nothing like having a friendly lunch with people who just smashed your breasts like pancakes every which way to keep you humble!

I had worked in medical transcription for nearly 15 years and had transcribed more mammograms than I could count at that point. So it came as no cause for concern really when I got the phone call that they wanted to do a repeat mammogram with possible ultrasound the next day. This is a fairly normal occurrence and while I was a little nervous about it, I honestly didn't think it would be a big deal.

As I walked down for my appointment the following day, suddenly I felt a lump in my throat, a tightness in my gut and a moment of panic. As I walked into the room, I was met with a familiar and friendly face to reassure me. She explained they just wanted to double-check a couple of areas that looked a little questionable. She explained this was routine and I nodded and expressed I understood.

She took a few more spot compression images and politely said she would show the radiologist to see if he wanted an ultrasound as well. I sat in the chair with my front opening gown on, now feeling more nervous than before. I felt my knee bouncing up and down as I sat up and tried to tilt my head side to side to relieve some of the tension building up between my shoulders. As the friendly face returned she said the radiologist would like to do an ultrasound as well. Looking back, I recall how soothing she was in her voice and how she did everything she could to make me feel at ease and not let the anxiousness overcome me.

I laid back on the ultrasound table and took a deep breath.

"What do they see?" I thought to myself over and over.

The radiologist came in the room and peered over the ultrasound tech's shoulder. There was some pointing at the screen and a few "Mmm-hmms" and "there, and there". I started to feel like a sideshow. I felt too nervous to ask what they saw, so I kept quiet until I was instructed to sit back up.

"I'd like to send you down to UW Madison to have a biopsy." The radiologist said in a calm yet concerned voice. "You have so many microcalcifications, in both breasts, that I am not able to count them all."

"Oh. Okay. Um, how do I do that?"

"The receptionist will take care of it, and you should hear from UW Madison in a couple of days with your appointment."

A biopsy? Suddenly, even though I had transcribed "microcalcifications" probably hundreds of times, I couldn't remember the meaning of the word and what it actually meant. I had a jolt of panic run through me as I got dressed and headed back upstairs to work. I felt like my brain was not fully comprehending what just happened.

I picked up my phone and text my husband, "they want to do a biopsy in Madison! WTF?"

Waves of fear, panic and numbness took turns over the next few days until my phone rang. A pleasant woman on the other end greeted me.

"Hello Mrs. Babcock, I'm looking to get you scheduled

for several biopsies. Looks like they are wanting five, which is unusual. They've never done five biopsies in one day." She explained with a curious tone in her voice.

"Oh? I thought it was just one. Yikes!" I nervously laughed trying to pretend she didn't just scare the shit out of me.

I took down the date and time and wrote down all the instructions.

"NOW WHAT?" WAS ALL I COULD THINK

Interestingly, I tried to play it off as no big deal to my friends and family. For the most part, I really tried to ignore it myself. But the Saturday before my appointment I was home alone and had the realization that this could be breast cancer. After all, my father's side of the family was riddled with it. Most, if not all, of his female cousins, had breast cancer and my aunt passed away from it at age 50. The heaviness of that reality weighed on me. I felt the pressure behind my eyes build up. Once the tears started, I just let it all out and sobbed sitting there by myself on the couch.

The day of the appointment, the radiologist came in and explained that five biopsies were a lot to do in one day. She told my husband and me that their team of radiologists had met about my case. They came to the conclusion that they would just perform one biopsy that day and see what the results were and go from there. She said between the cost and potential pain from the procedure, this was the better route to go. All in all, the procedure wasn't terrible. It was a little uncomfortable and I had some discomfort afterwards, but for the most part, it wasn't bad at all. The waiting that came after was worse than the actual procedure. Every time my phone rang, I was hoping it was the hospital calling with my results.

Just after getting home one night, my phone rang. The caller ID showed up as UW Madison Hospitals and Clinics and I froze. As much as I wanted to hear my results, I also didn't want to hear them at the same time.

"Hello?" I answered.

"Is this Wendy?" a voice on the other end asked.

"Yes, this is she."

"Hi, Wendy, this is the radiologist from UW Madison. Your biopsy results came back benign."

Suddenly a huge sigh of relief came over me. She explained it was good news, but also explained that it would be a good idea for me to have genetic testing done due to my extensive family history of breast and other cancers.

The next phone call I'd have to wait for was from the geneticist. In late January 2016, I was told I was BRCA2 positive. When the word "positive" came through the phone, I didn't hear anything else she said. I was sitting in my car in the parking lot of the restaurant my husband worked at and I sat there for what seemed like forever just staring into space feeling numb.

"Now what?" was all I could think. Now, what do I do? I had already gone over my options with the geneticist. I knew I could continue to do watchful waiting, which meant every six months I would alternate a mammogram with an MRI. I knew my risk of breast cancer was around 85%. I knew the anxiety I felt while waiting for the results of the biopsy and the genetic results that waiting wasn't exactly my forte. I've always been a terribly impatient person and I just could not imagine myself waiting for a result every six months. And in that moment, I also knew what my choice would be...surgery.

I spent the next month joining social media groups for women who were BRCA positive. I searched online to figure out if I'd want to go flat, have implants, or if there was another alternative. I started to come across women talking about having DIEP flap reconstruction. This meant I would have reconstruction using my own tissue and not implants. As soon as I knew that was an option, I felt it was exactly what I would want. I had my list of questions, concerns and knew a lot about the procedure I wanted when I met with the plastic surgeon. He seemed a little surprised at the homework I had done. He called it the "Ferrari of reconstruction surgery". It was a longer, more extensive surgery, but it was also basically a one-and-done surgery. With implants, most often, you have expanders placed. Then you make several trips back in to have those filled until you're able to have the actual implants placed. It also sounded like the implants would need to be switched out in about 10 years. I just didn't want to have to go through with any of that. I opted for the DIEP flap surgery. The surgeon explained how after the breast surgeon did her part, then he would come in and cut me from hip to hip and basically take a football shape incision out of my abdominal fat. This would be used to reconstruct new breasts. After the surgery, because it is my own tissue, my new breasts would lose and gain weight with the rest of my body. They would be the same temperature as my body as well. Of course, this surgery came with more potential complications including failure of the new tissue to thrive. It was also a longer surgery and a harder recovery, but my mind was made up and I was ready. The funniest part was that normally during the surgery, due to the abdominal tissue taken, a new belly button would need to be reconstructed as well. I just did not see any point in that. In my eyes, it was just another place for a potential postop infection. I read so many occurrences of this in the social media groups I was in, so I told him, thanks but no thanks. He looked quite puzzled at me and said no one had ever requested not to have their belly button reconstructed. We had a good laugh, but I knew what I wanted. My surgery was scheduled for April 11, 2016.

I woke up feeling groggy, confused and nauseous with my family standing at the end of the bed looking at me with excited faces. I interpreted that as my surgery went well and I closed my eyes again. The next thing I remember was the nursing staff and CNAs coming in every 15 minutes with a Doppler device to check the blood flow of the new breast tissue. The left side was a dark purple color all over and the nursing staff seemed quite concerned. By the second day, I started to feel really out of sorts. I could not focus my eyes and felt like my heart was racing. My heart rate started to set the alarms off in my room. The nursing staff rushed in, checked everything very calmly and reassured me. They ran some lab tests which showed I'd lost a lot of blood during the 12-hour surgery and I would need a blood transfusion. The surgery was supposed to be around eight hours, but there was a complication in finding a specific artery and they really had to dig around on the left side, thus the diffuse purple bruising on that side. This lead to my surgery being 12 hours.

Once the blood transfusion started, I almost immediately began to feel better. I cannot say enough wonderful things about the team that took care of me at this hospital. They were all so kind, compassionate, patient and professional. I had 9 drains when I came out of surgery. Fortunately, when I was ready to be discharged, they were able to take four of them out.

THE HEALING PROCESS

I was not at all expecting to see the "old me" when I looked in the mirror. While at the hospital, I had only caught glimpses of what I looked like and was not able to fully absorb it. Coming home was definitely a challenge both physically and emotionally. I fully expected the physical challenges, but the emotional challenges took me completely off guard.

I did my homework. I read the personal stories of women who had this same procedure done and what their reactions were to seeing themselves fully naked in the mirror. I felt like I had done so much research, looked at photos and truly listened to so many personal stories, that I honestly thought I'd be completely prepared for what I would see.

The pouch of fat from having children and gaining weight I was accustomed to was gone. In its place was a long incision from one hip to the other, pulling very tightly on the skin connecting my pubic area and my abdominal area. There was no belly button and I was unable to stand up straight. My left breast was still a dark purple. I hadn't seen my breasts look that firm ever. They were swollen and looked almost square. Where my nipples used to be were now circular scars with two straight lines extending from each side on both breasts. The drains that were still attached to my right hip and under my arms had bright red fluid in them.

Staring at the mirror felt surreal. I knew it was me, but yet, I felt as though I was somehow in someone else's body. I got angry at myself. After all, I knew what to expect. Why was I so shocked? Why did I break down and cry not knowing who the hell was staring back at me in the mirror?

During the healing process, I had a moment that I honestly thought I was going to die. Not even two weeks before my surgery, I received devasting news that my younger cousin, a mere 38 years old, died from a postoperative infection. She had been diagnosed with breast cancer that Fall and had underwent a bilateral mastectomy. She, too, was diagnosed with BRCA2 gene mutation. She had also opted for a total hysterectomy, which was performed that January. Somehow, even after getting the all-clear to return to regular activities, she developed an infection, became septic, and passed away.

It was at the point in my healing when I only had one drain left. It was on my right hip. I noticed upon getting out of the shower that something was draining out of the incision site and coming out in copious amounts. The incision site was red and ached a bit. I had been feeling under the weather and thought I just had a cold. Immediately upon realizing the incision site was infected, I had a full melt-down panic attack. I had to wait about ten minutes to call my surgeon's office so I could calm down enough to talk. They told me to come right in. The next call was to my husband who made it home in record time. As the surgeon expressed the gunk from my abdomen, I couldn't help but cry. She stopped briefly and asked if it was painful and I told her no, it didn't hurt but explained I was just scared due to what happened to my cousin. She understood and I just laid there holding my husband's hand and cried. Obviously a strong antibiotic and a little more draining and I fully recovered.

Physically, I was making progress. I did my physical therapy as instructed and rested. I was released to go back to work as well. But something still wasn't right. I was falling deeper into a depression. I couldn't focus at work. I felt myself distancing from friends and family. Every time I looked in the mirror, I felt "blank". I didn't feel like me anymore. And if we're being real, when it came time, I had no desire for sex. I didn't feel sexy or attractive at all. It was like looking at a Barbie doll, minus the thin, yet curvy figure, but just...blank. All I could see were scars. Regardless of how much my husband reassured me that he was definitely attracted to me and told me I was beautiful, I just didn't feel it. I started to dread looking in the mirror. I started to get more and more depressed. I would lay awake after my husband fell to sleep and cry. I didn't know who to talk to and didn't want anyone to know how much I had been suffering. I felt like I was being judged anyway for having done this more extensive surgery. Sometimes I felt as if there were whispers behind my back that it was vain to want reconstruction done. No one ever said anything like that to my face, but it was something I just felt deep down. Maybe it was my own lack of self confidence at that point. I just wanted to look as much like "normal" as I could.

MY PHOTOSHOOT

Late in 2016, I came across a social media post from an old friend who did boudoir photography. She was looking for someone who had tattoos to do a boudoir session with her. I remember looking at that post over and over and feeling like I should apply. But at the same time, I felt like I looked like Frankenstein. Yet, for some reason, I finally did submit the application for her model call.

When I got the email back from her that she chose me, I was shocked and excited. It was the first time in months I felt like I had something to really look forward to. We had a wonderful consultation where she told me how the sessions worked and what to expect. She showed me some fun lingerie she had available and I got to pick something out from a catalog just for my photoshoot.

When the day arrived, she took me out for coffee and then to a lovely salon where I felt super pampered and had my makeup and hair professionally done. I was not used to being fawned over like that. But it was such a fun experience.

When we got back to her studio, she helped me get changed and walked me through posing. It felt a little awkward but her energy was so comforting that those feelings didn't last long. I couldn't wait to see my pictures!

Something interesting happened that day. I felt pretty. I felt sexy. I felt like "me" again. I had no idea answering that model call that this would happen. It made me even more excited to see the finished product.

When my husband and I returned to pick up the photos, I was really nervous. What if I looked fat? What if I hated them? Thankfully that wasn't the case. It wasn't the look on my husband's face as I watched his eyes light up at what he saw. It wasn't the excitement I watched as he turned each page and seeing me posed in dramatic ways. It was my own reaction to the photos that surprised me the most. As I looked at myself, I actually saw myself. It was like the pieces of me that had been missing for months had suddenly been placed in front of me. I could see a glimpse of the scars peeking out from the lingerie and I felt proud. That was ME!

While it took me a while to understand why this photoshoot had such a profound effect on me emotionally, I finally think I know what it was. It was like I was finally able to see myself through someone else's eyes. I had been staring at myself in a mirror and wondering where I had gone. Then, without warning, I had the perspective of another person on the other side of the camera. My depression started to lift. My energy started to flow back in. And yes, my husband appreciated the new feelings I had of being attractive and sexy.

And that wave of emotion that knocked me over months before finally calmed and guided me back to shore. The storm had passed.

ACKNOWLEDGMENTS

From the bottom of my heart, I'm forever grateful to my husband Brian and my daughters Jennifer and Kaitlin. They stood with me this entire journey! Their encouragement, love and support made all the difference! Love you all! And to Becky Plautz for helping me find myself again through her amazing photography session.

ABOUT AUTHOR

Wendy Babcock is an overcomer. Life has thrown a lot her way like childhood and domestic abuse in which she felt as though she lost herself. She is a firm believer that God has a purpose for everything and this journey is what helped her discover her true self. As a mother of two incredible young women, Wendy has strived to continue learning about communication and personal development in order to strengthen her relationships with her girls. Wendy is happily married to her husband Brian who has been a pillar of support throughout all her emotional and entrepreneurial endeavors.

ABOUT MY BUSINESS

Wendy Babcock is the founder of SLAM Networking, which encourages entrepreneurs and business owners to SLAM the door on outdated networking, SLAM the door on inauthenticity and SLAM the door on boring & mundane superficial conversations! She has created a SLAM Networking Journal to help track and monetize connections. Wendy has also pioneered the Profit Up Expert Emporium, which is a virtual mall of experts for newish entrepreneurs looking to gain knowledge of all the foundational skills they need to be successful and bring their profits up!

Website
Http://wendynetworks.com

Facebook Personal Page
Http://Facebook.com/wendybabcockpresents

Instagram
Http://Instagram.com/wendybabcock_networks

THANK YOU

As a thank you, I would love to invite readers to connect with me inside my amazing SLAM Networking community- the Neighborhood.

I'd like to gift you 30 days free. Please use coupon code FIRST27. Http://slamhappyhour.com

Karen Clarke-Hoffmann

THE HAND I WAS DEALT
My Journey With Infertility, From Broken To Awesome

I am 26 and I avoid family gatherings – because the first thing aunties and cousins ask, is when am I getting married – "You are getting on in life you know." Or "You don't want to be left on the shelf" It doesn't matter that I have a thriving career and bought my own house 4 years ago – age 22 – NO that is totally irrelevant! The fact that I'm not married and 26 – now apparently that is newsworthy! (and btw – my male cousin who is also 26 and unmarried does not get judged because "he is a man and is enjoying his life!")

So, in April 2000 I packed my bags, rented out my house and moved to London! I will never forget – when the plane took off from Johannesburg Airport, as we left South African soil – I knew with complete certainty in my heart and mind that I will never again live in South Africa. Even though I only had a 2 year visa – but those are details right? You don't worry about details like that at 26!

And yes, you predicted correct – In February 2002, I met the love of my life in London – in a bar nevertheless - 6 weeks before my visa ran out! I had to go back to South

Africa for a couple of weeks to apply for a work permit - love conquered all and end of May 2002 I moved back to London!

On a bright Saturday afternoon in April 2005 Dad walks me down the aisle in a small church in the heart of Devon in the UK – Karl and I had a small wedding with only 50 close friends and family. It was the only sunny day that April. In Africa, the belief is, if it rains on your wedding day – you will be fertile and blessed with many children. April. Sunny day. Not even an April shower the entire day. Mmmmmm....just saying!

At least now everyone can get off my back – how wrong was I. We've hardly said our "I Do's", the ink is still wet on our marriage certificate – when the questions start again – "When are you having children? You are not that young anymore, you know". I am 31 for heaven's sake – oh did I mention I have a very successful career at GE – Yes me – the one nobody ever expected will be successful – just get married and have babies they said, and frankly that's all I ever wanted – this career thing was never part of the plan – not my plan anyway! But here I am rocking the career thing!

A year later we buy a house in the Home Counties, in a town called Woking – about 40 miles outside of London and only 25 minutes to London on the fast train – because the "plan" is for me to continue working in London when Junior comes. But a year later there is still no sign of Junior. The room that is going to be the baby's room is still empty.

Now we have to endure comments like: Don't you guys know how to do it? Do we need to show you? We can buy you a book?

God, what's wrong with people?

And the advice we received. One of my favorites - After you had sex – put your legs up against the wall to give the sperm a chance to get upstream to your eggs! Really?

I know you are probably thinking what bloody idiots did we hang out with? But I kid you not – that was what a family member's wife advised me – thank God she is not a blood relative! I would have had to scrape her from the family tree.

You are not deemed as having issues to conceive or infertile at age 33 – you are apparently still too young and should just keep on trying.

Me being me – I followed my gut – I pushed the issue and our super invasive rollercoaster journey started – looking back if I knew what was coming, I might have just accepted the hand I was dealt with sooner – or not, because there is always: "what if" but hindsight is a great thing, right?

WHY GOD, WHY?

First, they have to make sure I have no endometriosis or blocked tubes – so I am booked for surgery – turns out no blocked tubes – but my ovaries and womb are covered with endometriosis. I got the all clear. We are encouraged to go on a vacation to relax and hopefully conceive – so off we go to Cuba! Beautiful beaches, bright blue ocean – we relax, have fun, enjoy ourselves. We love Havana and buy a Cuban cigar for when our baby is born (a few years later we gave that cigar to my cousin's husband when her first baby is born) – but two days before the end of the holiday – my period arrives! Yet again, we are both devastated.

Time to get Karl checked out when we get home. He gets booked in with one of the top urologists in the country – and a very invasive and painful surgery follows. I remember helping him shower the day after the surgery – I started laughing and said to him: I thought it will be at least another 40 years before I have to shower you!

After he got the all clear – it is now apparent that natural conception is not an option for us.

The rollercoaster of IVF continues! We are sent to see one of the trailblazers in the IVF field in the UK – at least he is excited about our case. It's another long appointment – where we go over our history AGAIN – every time we see a new doctor it opens up a lot of emotions, it's draining, it's raw, I cry, Karl withdraws into himself. I have a lot of questions – why us? Is it worth it? But we really want a family? Should we persevere?

After several more appointments and consults our case is approved – and the wait to start our IVF begins – the wait can be anything up to 18 months. We are exhausted – and decide to go on vacation to Florida to visit Karl's cousin and his family (who is his godparents and Karl is the godfather to their son and he will be the godfather to our baby) – whom I've never met – like I need more stress in my life! But we go – and it was a Godsend! I get along with them from the word go. We talk for hours – I open my heart to his godmother, Bronwyn, – we cry together, she encourages me and gives me hope. This is also the vacation I do my first triathlon – yes – who goes on vacation and does a triathlon – me apparently! I fell in love with the sport and in the months and years to come it was a lifeline for me.

After 10 amazing days, we head home – as we board our flight at Tampa Airport – I said to Karl: Maybe our letter to start IVF is waiting for us at home – wouldn't that be great? Always the realist Karl tells me not to get my hopes up! For once he was wrong – when we got home our letter is waiting – we need to make an appointment at the Queen Mary Hospital in Roehampton – so we did and we had to wait months for the appointment – apparently having issues to conceive is rather common these days!

The day of our appointment arrives - a gray, cold, autumn morning – we have the first appointment of the day – we are quiet as we drive to the hospital, I'm so nervous I can't even laugh at the jokes off my favorite morning D.J.

After yet another long draining appointment we leave the hospital with a plan that will kick into action after my next period. We go over the side effects and risks of IVF, what to expect during the next couple of months, Do's and Don'ts, the harvesting of the eggs – my head is spinning.

Karl drops me off at Richmond station to get the train into London and we go to work – because that's what we do - this will become our routine over the months to follow. I'm a bit of a mess when I get to work - my boss gives me one look and sends me home – for once I don't argue and I go home.

All these emotions – I'm nervous, I'm scared, I fight with God – surely it shouldn't be this difficult to have a baby – the one thing I always wanted in life. Karl and I both have so much love to give we have so much to offer a child – why God, why? Why us? You see 16 year old girls walk down the High Street with a pram – why them? I'm in constant battle with God, but at the same time, I'm clinging to my faith.

Karl clears his schedule for the next few months – no traveling. We are in this together, it's our journey, he wants to be by my side every step of the way – I love him even more.

The next few weeks is pure hell. I have to spray this stuff up my nose three times a day that is shutting down my reproductive system – I'm basically putting myself through menopause. I have hot flushes, I'm emotional, I cry for no reason.

Then the injections start – and if I think the first part was hell – this is worse. I have to inject myself every day at a specific time. My upper legs are bruised from the injections. Karl is quiet and later shares with me how helpless he felt – seeing me going through all this and he couldn't do anything. But his support means the world to me – knowing he is there when I inject myself, driving me to our doctor's appointments 3 times a week.

I'm the poster child for women going through IVF – no alcohol, no caffeine, no strenuous exercise, if the doctor said I shouldn't do it – I don't do it!

Three times a week I'm at the Queen Mary at 7:30am – I get prodded and scanned – I would years later jokingly say to my Gynecologist – I've had IVF, my legs automatically open whenever I see a doctor!

My results are not what they should be. My hormone dosage is increased the last week before the harvesting of the eggs – I feel rotten, I'm exhausted. I'm fighting with God. I'm pleading with God – please make this work – please let us have a baby.

I'm not the only one going through hell. Karl is having his own battles. He feels helpless seeing me going through all this. Injecting myself. My legs are blue. But he doesn't show it – he is my rock.

The day of my egg harvest arrives – a Wednesday – I take the rest of the week off work. Karl drives me to the hospital. I will be put under a light anesthetic, they will harvest the eggs, Karl will then take the eggs up to Guy and St. Thomas Hospital in London where he will make his contribution and the eggs will be fertilized. We have it all planned out and manage to find humor in the situation – Karl having a "team talk" with his sperm and being allowed to watch porn!

I remember walking into the operating theatre where the harvesting will take place (I was a bit shocked that I had to walk into the theatre and that I wasn't wheeled in) – the anesthetist was playing: 'Special start that shines', by the South African band Mango Groove.

All goes according to plan.

I get a call from the Fertility Centre the next day – I only had two eggs. They fertilized both. One didn't make it. The other one is developing fast and needs be to implanted ASAP. Friday morning at 11am I will be impregnated. I allow myself to be a little excited.

On our way to the Fertility Centre – we walk past a beautiful Cathedral – We go inside and light a candle for our baby.

It was surreal – we watch on a screen how I'm being

impregnated – they give me a sonar picture of our baby. Two weeks later the pregnancy test confirms it. God granted my wish – we are going to have a baby. We keep the news to ourselves for a few days – we want to enjoy this bliss, this miracle for just a few days.

We dream. We plan. We think of names. I love being pregnant.

6 weeks later for my birthday, Karl gives me the most beautiful Gucci necklace as a thank you for what I endured so we can have a baby. The next day I started bleeding. Just spotting at first. The doctor tells me to stay in bed, this is not uncommon. I stay in bed – I am not losing this baby. Enzo (my cat) never leaves my side. I do at least one pregnancy test a day to make sure I'm still pregnant – I'm obsessed. I'm scared. I pray. Thursday, November 21, I am doubled over in pain. I call the doctor again – I'm told to go to the Early Pregnancy Centre (or something like that – that week was a blur) at St. Peter's hospital – they are open until noon, it's 11:15am! Somehow, I managed to drive myself the 5 miles to the hospital and find parking. I get lost in the hospital – I walk by a room where the machines connected to an old man is beeping like crazy – strange what I'm remembering of that day. I finally find the place where I need to be – I check-in and go to the toilet to do a urine sample – as I sit down on the toilet. The most gut-wrenching pain shoots through me and I miscarry, right there in the toilet of St. Peters hospital - alone.

A scan confirms my loss.

I walk out of the hospital. I'm empty. My heart aches. I'm angry at God. I get home, crawl into bed, cuddle Enzo and cry myself to sleep. Later when Karl gets home, we cry together for the loss of our unborn baby. Our beautiful baby.

WHAT NOW?

There are no words that can describe a miscarriage, the loss of life, the loss of your baby. Nothing could prepare me for the days, weeks, months, and years that followed. Before and during IVF there is hope – hope of a baby. Now, there is nothing – not even hope. The bruises on my legs from the injections eventually fade and finally disappears. I'm broken. The emptiness, the hopelessness, the loss, however, does not fade or disappear.

I go back to work the following Monday – hoping that being busy will take my mind off my loss and help me heal. I am on autopilot and just go through the motions. There is no joy in anything I do – I smile when I'm expected to smile and bury myself in my work.

Super exhausted, drained, and empty, we drive to Chamonix on December 26 to go skiing – we ski one of Europe's most challenging areas for 10 days – the first ski lift up, last run down. Surely this will help us forget, take away the pain, make us whole again.

We start the next year with the intention to move forward to make peace with our loss. I attend baby showers of friends and the christening of their babies – it hurts like hell – but I do it – because it's "expected" of me. Many people know what we went through – you think they would have sympathy or at least keep quiet about having a family. At one christening I'm cuddling the baby of the moment – when a distant family member walks up to me – full well knowing what I went through the previous year, and with a smirk on her face says to me: "It suits you". I look at her puzzled as I had no idea what she meant. Seeing the look on my face – her smirk grows wider, and she points to the baby saying: "A baby in your arms – it really suits you". Somewhere I found the strength not to drop the baby or to slap the smirk off her face.

I start building a wall around me – nothing baby related or child related. If I meet people with young children – I do not pursue a friendship – I want nothing to do with pregnant friends or family, newborn babies or young families. I send gifts to the baby showers, birth and christening – but I do not attend.

I met Hayley Anderson cycling with our cycle club one Sunday morning – we ride together. Hayley is awesome – but she has 2 young daughters – according to my rule I cannot pursue this friendship! But Hayley is having none of that! As a fellow South African she is direct and straightforward – not to mention persistent! We became great friends and I adore her daughters – becoming an honorary aunt. I believe that is when the healing started - thanks to Hayley and her girls. (Hayley sadly passed away from cancer in October 2019 – I was blessed to see her a month before she went to heaven and thank her for not giving up on me)

FINDING MY PEACE

Fast forward a couple of years – in 2014 we move to California – new friends, new neighbors, new work colleagues – and then all the questions start again! I have my standard answer ready: "We were not blessed with children". The Americans, however, do not ask further questions nor do they say things like "well, you are still young there is time" or "don't give up hope" – they let it go! And I love them for that!

My battle with God continues. But God is persistent! He sends more angels my way. He leads me to Menlo Church – where with the guidance of Pastor John Ortberg – my faith is slowly restored.

August of 2017, we spend a wonderful few days with our dear friends, Dan and Jennifer Lahl, at their vacation home on Lake Tahoe.

One afternoon Jennifer and I are sitting on the dock sipping wine – the lake is peaceful and beautiful. I tell her my story and about my battle with God. When I'm finished Jennifer says to me: "Maybe it's time you stop fighting with God and start thanking Him". I'm confused – did I hear her correctly? What is there to thank God about? Not only did He not bless me with children – he took away my baby.

Then Jennifer explains: "Has it ever occurred to you that you or Karl has a disease or something you don't even know about and that can only be transmitted to a child through birth? Or that your baby might have been deformed."

And like that – overlooking the beautiful lake Tahoe – I find my peace after many, many years of battle.

I do not know why God did not bless us with children, it does not matter to me anymore. I do know that God has blessed Karl and I in many other ways.

I will never be whole again – at this moment in time I am as whole as I will ever be again – and it is okay – no, it is more than okay – I am awesome, living an awesome life with my awesome husband - every day I choose to make awesome out the hand I was dealt.

ACKNOWLEDGMENTS

Big thank you to Karl – my rock, my biggest cheerleader and my sparing partner. Thank you for always pushing me that little bit further, challenging me to answer those difficult questions, for getting me out of my comfort zone and most of all thank you for loving me the way I am.

ABOUT AUTHOR

After living on 3 continents – my husband Karl and I, made San Carlos, a small town in the heart of Silicon Valley California, our home, where we live with "our zoo" - two cats, Harry and Enzo and our labradoodle called Sprocket! I love being active and exploring – from hiking in the hills surrounding our house to paddle boarding and swimming with Sprocket. The beach is my happy place – it's where I go to get grounded, breath and recharge when live gets too hectic! With Karl life is an adventure – he is continuously encouraging me to do random activities – including surfing, skiing and very recently E-foiling! (Google it – it is fun!) Being part of a community is very important to me – and I have aspirations of being Mayor of San Carlos some day!

ABOUT MY BUSINESS

As a realtor, I cover all aspects of residential real estate. I help first time home buyers get into the market, growing families find larger properties, seniors downsize and investors cash flow. My previous career experience in financial service, supply chain management and business development has provided me with negotiation, financial and people skills necessary! I'm very people focused in my business approach – it's my goal to help my clients find a physical sense of belonging. Along with my fulfilling work in real estate – I have a passion for health and fitness. I am a qualified Personal Trainer and Wellness Coach. I inspire women to gain body confidence and support them on their journey. Taking a holistic approach to lifestyle, exercise, attitude and nutrition to become the best version of themselves.

Website
www.karenhoffmann.biz

Facebook Personal Page
https://www.facebook.com/karen.clarkehoffmann

THANK YOU

Thank you for reading my story – if I can support you in any way or if you just fancy connecting – I'd love to hear from you!

Ingrid Dick

I JUST WANT YOU TO KNOW WHO I AM

THE ILLUSION OF "BEFORE"

Yeah, yeah, you know this narrative. Once upon a time there was a cool chick, Me. She was happy, or so she thought, living her life, raising kids, immersed in family activities, community service, and youth sports: she was the ultimate supermom.

Then something big happened. Like, really big. So now life is divided into two categories: life "before" the trauma, and who she was then, and life "after" - the character she embraces and identifies with now. It's such a cliche, right? The dichotomy of before and after and the grief and loss that goes along with it.

Let's talk about the concept of "before". It's the past. That's it. Game over. Gone, baby, gone! It no longer exists. We can recall our memories of it, but this is actually an illusion. Why? Because we are not physically there anymore! We are not remembering what exactly transpired, but rather our own fantastic version of it. It's not real, it's more like a dream.

The more time that passes, the more my "before" feels like a dream. It's almost like it happened to another person, or in a past life. It no longer feels real. It no longer defines me, and it certainly no longer triggers me. I've moved on. I'm not that person anymore. I've let that shit go.

So why do we spend so much time reliving the past? To the point where not letting go of our baggage makes us sick? Rehashing those past conversations and interactions, agonizing over choices made, and the "what ifs". It's so utterly pointless. We can't ever go back and make a different choice, say different words, turn left instead of right.

Now I understand how it all transpired, the perfect storm that summoned up this strange and deadly illness: how I ultimately manifested it in its entirety. My doctors performed cutting edge genetic testing on me, yet they still say can't say for sure what caused my disease. But I know. I may not have gone to medical school, but I know my body better than anyone.

One of the fundamental concepts of Ayurveda is that all disease has a cause, and that 90% of chronic illness can be prevented. This really resonated with me. I see now that it was the accumulation of a lifetime of poor judgments, missed opportunities, bad timing, and regret, partnered with horrible lifestyle choices, low self-esteem, negative self-talk, and the inability to set healthy boundaries. This set me on the dark path that almost killed me.

Am I the same Ingrid I was "before" the disease? No. That woman no longer exists, except in my memories.

She's not real, not anymore, that Ingrid is a shadow. But she sure taught me a lot! I'm grateful for her.

What's so special about my story? Am I just another exhausted, bored, minivan-driving housewife, who embarked on some kind of miraculous transformation? A cliche right? Well, here's the thing about cliches - there is a nugget of truth to them. This is my truth. What is yours?

AND SO, IT BEGINS

What happened to me could happen to you. Maybe it already has. I hope not, because it sucked.

Let's travel back in time to the Fall of 2012. I had one kid in 2nd grade. My youngest was in kindergarten.

The holidays were rough. I was starting to experience some weirdness - random things that I couldn't explain. I would sweat profusely whenever I ate. I completely lost my sense of taste. Handfuls of hair would come out in the shower and be stuck to my pillow in the morning when I woke up. Rough ridges appeared on my fingernails. I put it down to stress, which as it turned out, was not altogether incorrect.

It was the end of January 2013. My husband took me out for dinner to celebrate my birthday. We went to my favorite local Michelin Star restaurant. It was divine. I felt very spoiled. Until the early hours of the next morning, when I became violently ill. We both ate the same food and drank all the same wines. My husband was fine, but I felt like I was dying.

Well, this was definitely not food poisoning. I figured

it must be Kindergarten stomach flu, and that I'd be fine in 24 hours or so. By the end of the week, I was sitting in my doctor's exam room, trying not to vomit all over him, and listening to his assessment that this was definitely not a bug I picked up from a bunch of 5-year-olds with dubious handwashing skills. And so, it began.

INVISIBLE ILLNESS: BUT YOU DON'T LOOK SICK

There's nothing quite like having a mystery illness to make you feel invisible. To be fair, there were some doctors who agreed that there was something seriously wrong with me, they just had no idea what. Even so, they passed me off on to the next person because they didn't have the time or inclination to deal with me. Unless they could diagnose me, prescribe a pill, or cut me open, they really weren't interested.

There were others, those specialists who never bothered taking a proper history, who barely spent 10 minutes with me. The ER doctors who pegged me as a drug seeker, patted me on the knee, and told me to "try to eat something, dear". There was one particularly obnoxious ER resident who made me feel so defeated because of her condescending tone.

For many of them, when they couldn't immediately identify what was wrong, they simply dismissed my symptoms as being a result of an overactive imagination and hypochondria. Because after all, I looked just fine. At least, on the outside, I seemed normal. On the inside, I was a disaster. I'll spare you the gory photos of my intestines.

To all my fellow chronic illness sisters and brothers out there, you know what I'm talking about. We are not faking being sick, we are faking being well. We go out into the world pretending to be OK, because when someone asks you the dreaded question, "how are you today?" God forbid you actually answer with the truth. Awkward! It's no fun being perceived as an attention-seeking drama queen.

For those of us who have had the misfortune of being awarded a lifetime membership to the chronic illness club, we've all been told "but you don't look sick!" or "Wow you look great, I wish I could lose weight like that! Maybe I can get your disease!" Trust me, it's one of the most demeaning and dismissive things you can say to someone who is genuinely struggling, and often in incredible pain. All I wanted was support, acknowledgment, and empathy.

Trying to get an initial consultation with a specialist doctor is super fun. There is no way, in this appalling sick-care system we are caught up in, to get an appointment to see anyone right away. The average is a 3-month wait. When I finally saw my first gastrointestinal doctor, I wasn't terribly worried at that early stage of things. This guy was a lot of fun. I liked him a lot. He was excited at the prospect of this possibly being a parasite, exclaiming that he "hadn't had a decent worm in months". Oh, if only it had been that simple!

I was sitting in his exam room for the follow-up after my first endoscopy to look at my stomach, when and he burst through the door, visibly flustered, and announced that he was "terribly sorry", but he needed to "go up the other end to take a look". He told me that he sees stomachs every day, and that mine looked like a hamburger. I'm pretty sure that wasn't normal. He wanted to see what the other end of me looked like. Let's just say, it was a disaster.

Such was my life that summer. I'd end up in the ER because of severe dehydration, thinking I just needed a bag of intravenous saline (IV) and I'd be fine, but then I'd collapse, and they would have to admit me because my metabolic labs were scary again and the pain was unbearable. Bring on the IV morphine. Let's just say that made my hallucinations worse. It also made me feel like I had fire ants crawling all over me, but that was still preferable to the pain in my belly. They ran bag after bag of IV meds. The potassium infusions were the worst. That shit burns. The nurses bought me ice packs and held my hand while I cried. In the end, I blew out all my veins, and they started examining my feet for possible entry points. Shit was getting real. I was scared, I won't lie.

By that point, I couldn't even keep water down, let alone any kind of solid food. I had been living on scrambled eggs for weeks. I had to keep paper bags in the car, so I could vomit into them when I was at the stoplights. Mostly by then, it was just constant dry heaving. I was constantly running to the bathroom. I didn't go out much. Thank God for my nanny. That spring and summer, I was the invisible mommy. I couldn't even take care of myself, let alone little kids. I lost a massive amount of weight because I was unable to absorb any nutrients.

The initial diagnosis was Crohn's Disease. We went back and forth on this. My local GI sent my biopsies to several different pathologists. They all agreed that it looked like Crohn's but observed that it was more like some kind of mutation of this disease. I had extreme inflammation in my entire GI tract, with hundreds of polyps from one end of me to the other. The pain was excruciating. It appeared as if aliens were growing inside of me. My doctor was completely stumped, and my situation dire. Honestly, I knew it was bad, but I never truly realized how close I was to dying at the time.

AND THE WINNER IS...

So, that's how I ended up in a state-of-the-art hospital and teaching facility in Southern California. It was the first day of school for my kids. My son was going into the 1st grade, my daughter the 3rd grade. My school mom friends were all flabbergasted to see my husband on campus dropping off the kids that day. I was already MIA, some of them knew I was sick, but I was always there, especially the week leading up to the start of the school year. Working the campus, greeting returning parents and students, welcoming the new arrivals, celebrating the teachers. Everyone was wondering what the heck was happening - speculating the worst possible scenarios. It had to be bad for me to miss the first day of school.

Meanwhile, back in San Diego, I was met at the concierge desk in the luxurious lobby of Thornton hospital by a wonderful woman who heads the Guest Relations department, and whom I immediately became friends with. They totally rolled out the red carpet for me, and I felt special. Finally, I was no longer invisible! And yes, I was a "guest", and they treated me like royalty. Unable to walk, or even stand without getting dizzy, they put me in a wheelchair and took me up to meet with my new doctor, the man who finally was able to solve my mystery illness, and who saved my life.

I was finally diagnosed with an extremely rare autoimmune disease called Cronkhite-Canada Syndrome. (CCS). CCS is a type of IBD (inflammatory bowel disease). There were only around 500 cases worldwide since the 1960s, at the time of my diagnosis in 2013. It has many similarities to Crohn's disease. It affects the entire GI tract and has a high mortality rate. Most patients either die of starvation, total organ failure, or cancer of the stomach or bowel. I was described as "metabolically bankrupt" and of being an "accidental anorexic". In the end, I didn't eat solid food for over 6 months, and basically lived on chicken broth. As an avid foodie, yes, I appreciate the irony. Thanks, universe!

I remember when he walked into the exam room. My new doctor was like a breath of fresh air. My heart skipped a beat. This was not the time to lose control of my bowels. He had already seen my previous lab work and scopes, and immediately put me at ease when he calmly looked in my eyes and announced he was certain that he knew what this was, and not to worry because he was going to take care of me. Finally! Afterwards, I wept. And so began the final round of poking and prodding to confirm what he suspected: Cronkhite-Canada Syndrome (CCS).

The next day I was wheeled into the OR for my scopes, feeling very nervous. I had not slept. My doctor confessed to me years later, that the first time he examined me and saw my small intestines up close, that the images he was seeing “took his breath away”. He claimed my small intestine was in the top 3 worst he had ever seen.

After a couple more days of additional tests, I was back in the ER, waiting to be admitted. They were almost sure of the diagnosis now, and my labs were worrying, showing a severe metabolic meltdown. The pain was monstrous. It was like being in labor, but in my guts, and it never let up. I’d had enough.

My veins were garbage. Chronic dehydration and endless infusions of potassium will do that. I’m still a hard stick all these years later. They set me up with a portacath, which is a small disc that is surgically implanted beneath the skin on the chest and used to gain venous access. So yay, no more painful IVs. I was tired of having tender, purple bruises up the entire length of my arm and the back of my hands. I ended up keeping that port for 5 years. It served me well. May it burn in hell.

The plan was to get me on TPN (total parenteral nutrition) so I could give my stomach and intestines a rest, and to feed me intravenously, because I was unable to absorb any nutrients. I was literally starving to death. My toenails peeled off, my hair fell out, and my gums bled. My feet and ankles swelled up, and I had to wear compression socks to prevent blood clots, and keep my legs elevated.

Once my portacath had been implanted, and now that I had a correct diagnosis, I started on TPN. Amazing how after just one 12-hour infusion I was able to get up and do a single lap around the nurse's station before collapsing again. After a couple of days, I was even feeling well enough to take a shower. That was pure bliss.

I went home after 9 nights in the hospital, armed with a suitcase full of TPN bags that the TSA scanned to make sure they weren't bombs, a shit load of steroids and narcotics, and something I never had before: hope.

THE ROAD TO RECOVERY: PART 1

Until me, T=there was no official treatment for CCS. My doctor came up with a new off-label protocol. I was the first CCS patient ever known to be treated with Remicade, a.k.a. Infliximab, which is given by IV infusion. I remember my first one, I sat there just breathing deeply, wishing the drugs to work, visualizing my intestines the way they are supposed to be - shiny, pink, and smooth. My goal was to eat a small Thanksgiving dinner of some turkey, mashed potatoes, and gravy. Maybe even a sip of wine.

Not only did I manifest the hell out of and enjoy that meal, but I was also able to wean myself off TPN fairly quickly. The following January, after 3 months, I went back to see my doctor for a re-check, and he couldn't believe the results. I was declared officially in clinical remission. All signs of the CCS was gone from my stomach and intestines. It was a miracle! I was feeling so much better. I could eat, I could play with my kids, I could pass a solid bowel movement. Things were looking up! I didn't know it at the time, but the expectation was at best, a 50% improvement of symptoms, with a 3-year life expectancy. This disease has a very high mortality rate. As I write this memoir, I'm going on 9 years of remission. But the best (and the worst) is yet to come.

For me, remission wasn't all it's cracked up to be. What does "remission" even mean? A stage of lesser intensity, when a disease subsides or improves. The thing is, I was still sick. Yes, I was technically in "clinical remission" and the disease had disappeared from my intestines, but I still had many symptoms, most of which I attributed as being side effects of the medications. Not the vomiting and diarrhea, or the pain in my guts, thank God that was gone, and I honestly felt better, but over time, I continued to experience plenty of other problems. Why? Because life returned to "normal". I had not changed!

Turns out I had learned nothing.

THE ROAD TO RECOVERY: PART 2

Post diagnosis and near-death experience, at first things were OK. I paced myself. Went to the spa. Took naps. But I was restless. This just wasn't me, sitting around all day. I had no purpose. I was bored, sad, and lonely.

You would think that this experience would be a wake-up call, right? Nope. As soon as the Remicade kicked in and I was no longer confined to my bed or stuck on the toilet, I got up and went right back to my old habits.

Did I exercise? Rarely. Maybe the odd walk around the park with a neighbor. Did I eat properly? Definitely not. Take-out was often on the menu. How about my sugar intake? I was a carb addict. Chips, ice cream and wine were my go-to comfort foods. What about sleep? I was a chronic insomniac, felt like a zombie by day. I binge ate, and I used food to deal with stress and anxiety. Any kind of real and genuine self-care was a rare occurrence. My weight ballooned out of control. I stopped caring. My stress levels were off the charts due to being a workaholic. Why? Seriously, why would a seemingly intelligent and sane person do this to themselves?

Looking back, I realize how completely crazy this was. It was my unhealthy, unbalanced lifestyle that caused my illness, and despite being given a second chance, I indulged in all this bullshit again.

THE FINAL CUT

Today, I have moved beyond clinical remission, reversed my disease, and live completely free of the debilitating symptoms of systemic inflammation, and crippling side effects from medications. I have been off Remicade for almost 3 years now. I consider my disease to not just be in remission - it's been completely reversed. I know it won't return. Why? Because I am not the same person I was "before". My life is completely different. And, most of all, I simply won't allow it. I refuse to let it back in.

While I completely recognize and acknowledge that Remicade, saved my life, I came to a point after 4 years, where I was no longer willing to accept that these drugs were a life sentence.

It was October of 2017. I was still in remission, but I felt lost. Defeated and depressed. That's when I received an amazing invitation to attend a women's goddess retreat in Kauai. I knew I had to go, there was just a feeling in my gut that this was going to change my life. I couldn't explain it. Plus, it's Hawaii, so yeah, they had me at "aloha". I had absolutely no idea what to expect.

That single decision changed my life.

It was at that retreat, with those incredible women, where I learned that I had tools at my disposal, whenever I needed them. I could conjure up a shield to deflect negativity and protect myself from external spiritual and emotional harm. I had a sword to cut through the crap and clear a path for me to achieve success, health, and happiness. I discovered that I possessed a cup that I must fill and drink from first, before I offer it to others - that self-care needed to be at the top of my list, rather than non-existent. I learned how to pacify my inner fire, to turn down the volume on the negativity, and to sit quietly and breathe, meditate, and heal peacefully. I learned that the only way out of this was to divert all this energy and transfer it to only good, positive, healthy behaviors. Otherwise, history would repeat itself.

Then came that one unforgettable night of our adventure, during the full moon. That pivotal moment, when time stood still, and the magic happened. It was raining. Not hard, more of misty, haphazard, and slightly sideways sprinkle. We stood on the beach, bathed in moonlight, soothed by the breeze. We were each gently and silently handed a plumeria flower. It was beautiful, so peaceful, and quiet. We all joined hands, in a sacred feminine circle, and envisioned that which was holding us back, the thing we wanted to, and needed to let go of most of all. Then, one by one, we made our way to the shore, our bare toes tickling in the moist sand, bent down, and gently dropped the delicate flower into the foamy breakers.

As I watched my bloom float effortlessly away, I uttered the words, and I truly meant them. I wanted to be free of the pain, and for the disease to be totally gone. My sisters on the beach were silent, but I felt their empathy, support, and solace as they held space for me that night. As I did for them. That was a powerful ritual. I knew in my gut, in my soul, that this was an epic manifestation, one that I would take with me back to the mainland. I had work to do. The Green Goddess was conceived that night.

REALIZING YOU ARE ENOUGH

Upon my return from Hawaii, I knew that things had to change. I didn't need a genius to remind me "the definition of insanity is doing the same thing over and over again and expecting different results". I no longer accepted that I had to live like this, and I was determined to find another way.

By this point, I had to take accountability for my part in the cause of my illness. All those negative thoughts and feelings I had about myself festered in my guts. I had no armor to deflect the excessive amounts of negativity that my dark and manic energy attracted, that was absorbed by my body and built up to the point that I started to rot from the inside out. I literally was so full of negativity, and I couldn't stop it from overflowing and oozing out of me, uncontrollably and repulsively.

It suddenly occurred to me that if I could manifest this disease, that I could just as easily make it GO AWAY! And so began the great un-manifestation, or rather, my regeneration.

I immediately went to work and did some research. After a lot of late nights and way too much overthinking, I decided to test out the popular Ketogenic diet, cutting gluten, grains, sugar, simple carbohydrates, and processed foods, therefore eliminating the systemic inflammation in my entire body. That was the hypothesis I set out to prove.

Within 3 days my symptoms were 80% improved. Wow, I think I'm on to something here! I was sleeping better, feeling less stressed, had no headaches, had more energy, my brain fog was lifting, my joints didn't hurt all the time, and incredibly, I was feeling happy!

For me, transitioning off my immune suppression medications and completely reversing this deadly illness was possible - by making significant lifestyle changes. Diet, meditation and exercise. Learning self-care, life balance, and how to let go of the things I cannot control, was a big part of this too.

I'LL HAVE WHAT SHE'S HAVING

Once people saw such a dramatic change in me, my weight loss, my renewed energy, my calm demeanor, they started asking what my secret was. I had requests from friends asking if I could help them overcome their own chronic health problems. Before long, I had an online support group.

Then it dawned on me that perhaps there was a purpose to my suffering. It became very clear to me that this journey was a lesson, one that I could pay forward to others. This illness, or rather my transformation, was what led me to my true calling.

I enrolled with the world's largest online health coaching school, the Institute of Integrative Nutrition, where I earned my health coach training. In 2020 I completed my certification as an Ayurveda Wellness Counsellor through Kerala Ayurveda Academy in Silicon Valley.

My coaching practice focuses on an integrative and holistic approach to health and healing. Sometimes, medical intervention including surgery and drugs, are necessary. It's all about making small changes over time, and finding a life balance the works for you. I can help with that. Why? Because I completely understand what you are going through. I've lived it. I've survived it.

BECOMING FABULOUS

Becoming fabulous is all about being present. The fear of the unknown can be crippling. We don't know what might happen, so we do nothing. This can have even worse consequences than making a mistake. Honestly, I don't even believe in the concept of mistakes. This is something

I teach in my workshops - that not getting the outcome you expected or hoped for is all part of the journey, and another opportunity for growth and learning.

The same goes for living in a future of fantasy, of what life could be like, if only… if only you got that promotion at work, if only you had the courage to ask that person out on a date, if only you lost 20 lbs. Stop daydreaming, and start taking action to get the things you want. Now! Do not pass go. Do not collect $200. Procrastination due to feeling overwhelmed is a tough one to overcome. How does one even start?

What led me to my final step to healing? How did I restore balance in my life? How did I escape the past, and change my destiny?

By understanding and identifying my WHY.
By being grounded firmly in the present.
By having clear intentions.
By being focused on realistic, timely goals.
By committing to making mindful choices every day and being open to new ways of doing things.
By manifesting a positive outcome.
By setting healthy relationship boundaries.

Change is scary but staying the same is scarier.

FINAL THOUGHTS

It was a long, challenging journey from the beginning of my symptoms to the present. I'm sharing with you the steps I took to overcome my invisible illness and regenerate into the fabulous woman, wife, mother, daughter, sister, aunt, friend, and coach that I am today.

This is what worked for me.

Maybe you are experiencing your own mystery disease, or invisible illness, - one of the many epidemics that plague our modern society. Hopefully, you will take something away from my teachings here and begin your own personal transformation.

I had the power in me the whole time, to heal, and to manifest the things I really want in life. I know this now. The power has always been within you too. Just pluck up the courage and go get it.

You are only one decision away from a completely different life.

Namaste.

POSTSCRIPT

I write only because
There is a voice within me
That will not be still

Please note, this is not meant to take the place of medical intervention or treatment. I advise you to seek a consultation with your health care provider before embarking on any exercise or dietary changes. Also, do not stop taking any of your prescribed medications without first consulting with your doctor. I worked closely with mine as I gradually weaned off my immune suppression therapy.

ACKNOWLEDGEMENTS

Lori Rose

ABOUT AUTHOR

COACH INGRID, THE DIABETES DIVA National Board Certified Health & Nutrition Coach Ayurveda Wellness Counsellor Motivational Speaker, Health Commentator Ingrid Dick is a dynamic and inspirational coach who helps women with Type 2 Diabetes reverse their disease, and work towards living a life free of medications and debilitating symptoms. After overcoming and reversing her own life threatening chronic illness, including a rare type of auto immune disease (IBD), Type 2 Diabetes, and Insulin Resistance, Ingrid has an intimate understanding of the challenges women face when trying to gain control of their health. Ingrid completed her training with the internationally renowned Institute for Integrative Health & Nutrition (IIN), is certified by the National Board for Health & Wellness Coaches (NBC-HWC), and received her Ayurveda certification from Kerala Ayurveda Academy. She has a thriving online coaching business, and currently has openings for new clients who are ready to embark on their own health transformation journey.

ABOUT MY BUSINESS

Ingrid's trainings and programs focus on an integrative and holistic approach to healing through nutrition and lifestyle. She specializes in helping people reverse their Type 2 Diabetes.

Website
www.greengoddess.guru

Facebook Personal Page
https://www.facebook.com/ingrid.dick

Instagram
https://www.instagram.com/coach_ingrid_green_goddess/

THANK YOU

I offer Free Strategy session. For a free health consultation, please email ingrid@greengoddess.guru or visit www.greengoddess.guru.

Nancy Towle

GOOD NEWS: THE PATTERN IS BROKEN!

Breaking The Patterns Of Allowing Abuse, Lack Of Control And Self Doubt

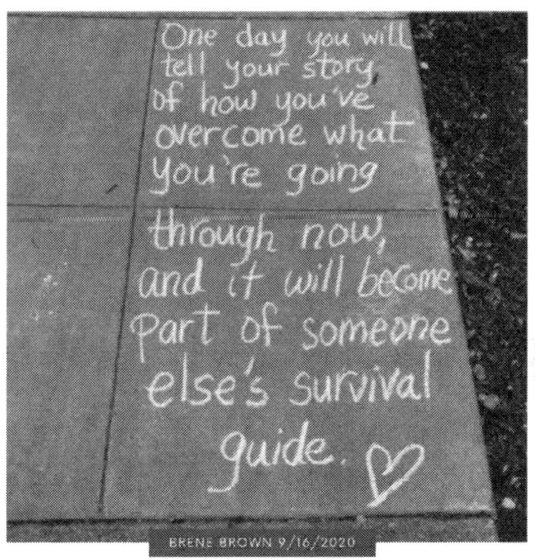

"Brene Brown"

As we look back over our lives introspectively, as if from a high peak, analyzing all of the highs and lows of life, looking carefully, we see patterns. Patterns of confidence and patterns of doubt and patterns of happiness and sorrow. You will see highs and lows and just certain things that keep coming back over and over. My pattern was continually being connected to those who wanted to control me AND at the same time were mentally or physically abusive. This is my story of those patterns of control and abuse that I did not even recognize much of the time and how I finally took my own control and BROKE THE PATTERN.

How did I finally come to this realization? I met an incredibly special personal coach in a networking organization I belong to. I listened to her talk many times as she introduced herself and told the group what she could do to help one become unstuck and how she did it. I scoffed deep inside.... who needs that? I did not know that I did! She was very intuitive and used her skills to read people's needs. I fought the desire to hire her because "I couldn't afford her". At one fateful networking meeting, she offered a one time $25 trial coaching session. I could never pass up a good deal and said yes, I'll give it a try. I was to "free form" type out the answers to 15 questions about my life and my feelings in advance. I sat down one night and following her direction, typed out 16 single spaced pages on a word document. I forwarded the pages to her the next day, met with her the day after, and from then on, my life was CHANGED! This woman read my long, long story in the form of her questions and when I arrived at our appointment, the first thing she said was "Good News, The Pattern is Broken". Believe it or not, I said "Oh really, what pattern is that?"

I honestly never allowed myself to look back to see

what my life looked like. I am forever indebted to this woman for the power she gave me. She gave me the freedom to walk away from those people who took control of me my whole life, mentally with those who were deceased and physically with those still living. I turned my back on these people, living and passed on, and eventually forgave them. She gave me the skill to see it in new relationships. She gave me the personal realization that I had the ability to break the pattern and moving forward, change my life!

I am a child of the '50s and '60s. Born later in the '50s, last of 3 girls, all 7 years apart. My mom had multiple miscarriages between each of us and by the time I came along, she was middle-aged. I always wondered if she really wanted me. A newborn with a 7 year old, a 14 year old and all girls!

My Mother was an orphan through most of her life until age 18. She lived in a facility with dorms and cafeterias and predominately "kids" that lost their parents during the two world wars. She never spoke of abuse or difficulties, but she and her 3 siblings had great emotional turmoil with the loss of both of their parents and no family able to take them due to the Depression. Each of her siblings led very difficult lives after leaving the orphanage, dealing with mental illness, alcoholism and addictions. Mom met my Dad at 18, got married at 20 and moved into the large family home that housed my Grandfather, Grandmother and two of my Dads siblings along with their wives and children. I hear my Grandmother was controlling, a little abusive and ran a tough ship. (I was born after all of my Grandparents had passed) Mom and Dad and my two sisters lived in that house until the year I was born when they moved into a house my dad built himself, just a few blocks from the Grandparents homestead.

My Mom ruled each of us with a look. If you got that look, you knew you were in trouble. She was under 5 feet tall and scared us to death with that look. I think she learned about running a tough ship from my Grandmother (her mother-in-law)

All three of us girls went to the local Catholic grade school attached to the family church and chapel. My Grandparents were very involved in the church and the building of it. They even had their names engraved on the stained-glass windows. I spent many hours in church looking at my distinctive childhood last name, up on those impressive works of art.

I could tell all the same stories others have of the Nuns and their use of "capital punishment". Rulers across the knuckles, writing multiple pages of the bible or the dictionary until your hands cramped and writing out "I will not talk in the hallways" 350 times. I think I was a smart child but just too afraid to show it. I struggled with moving between the Smart class, the Average class and what was known as the Dummy class. I moved between them until I decided it was just easier to stay in the dummy class. My parents actually said that was all they expected of me: (All their girls were quite average) (You only need to be smart enough to catch a good man, have babies and be a good cook) Those were the messages I received.

I LOOKED FOR APPROVAL

My patterns of being average and controlled and abused were set in stone in the middle of 3rd grade. President John F Kennedy promoted the "physical fitness" program in schools and since he was Catholic and we were Catholic, we were no longer going to have "Mom's" volunteer to play records for us to march around the gym and do pushups and sit-ups. In came Mr. T. Mr. T. was an Olympic gymnastics competitor who was hired to develop a fitness program for my school.

He did. He was incredible. My little school of 400 kids had a Gymnastic/physical fitness program like no other. We had Bars and Beams and Olympic sized trampolines, pommel horse, rings from the ceilings and we all learned how to use them! We had cheerleaders and pom-pom girls, Football, Baseball and basketball. He even had us put on two variety shows each year for the parents and the community. This man was revered right up there with Priests and Jesus. He could do no wrong. And, he molested hundreds of girls over his years at this school.

He was a fantastic athlete, great at organizing people, oozed charisma and was a pro at determining who he could take control over and make use of. He went after those girls that "needed" his attention whether it was because they wanted his ability to make you popular or when he determined you were ripe to be controlled by him due to your lack of self-esteem. He was a classic. He told me I wanted "it". He told me I asked him for "it". I was the "bad girl". My parents would never believe me if I told on him. He fed me these thoughts and warnings and I let him decide when he would kiss and touch and grab and press me up against the lockers in his office.

As you can guess, I never told anyone. I believed I was a "sinner", a "bad girl" and no one would believe me so it became my secret. I crammed it down into my soul so that I would not be ashamed every waking hour of my life. But I was ashamed because I sinned, I was not a great student, I was fat, I had pimples, I didn't keep my room clean enough, and on and on and on. (all but the sinning part came from my Mom…because that was her job to keep me from being proud of myself which was also a sin) In reality, I wasn't fat, I wasn't a slob, and I wasn't stupid. I know that now.

The gym teachers "taking advantage" continued until I graduated from 8th grade and my parents decided that since I was not a great student, why not send me to Public school instead of paying for Private School as they had with my sisters. I was the experiment! My four years of high school were very "normal". I looked for approval and it was difficult to find. I had friends in the mildly popular group, not the wildly popular group. My high school was in a very affluent area where most of the kids received cars on their 16th birthday. I walked to school all 4 years except on the special days when I could drive my Mom's 1969 Rambler in canary yellow. I had a serious boyfriend for two of the four years and we struggled with having each of our parents accept us because we came from different religious backgrounds. When college time rolled around, he went to one, I went to another and the relationship faded away. Maybe it was the underlying lack of self-esteem from my mother and the nuns and the gym teacher. I never really felt I belonged anywhere.

I was asked recently, who made the greatest impact on my life. There were a few but I had to say it was my high school counselor. She asked me during my Junior year, where I planned to go to college. I told her that my family did not go to college. No one had and probably no one would. I explained to her that my Dad felt college was a waste for a girl because she was only going to find a husband. (This was in 1973, not in the Dark Ages). This counselor, who was a proponent of "women's liberation" set up an appointment and went to my parents' home to convince my Dad that I should go to college and that I could be anything I wanted to be! She did a good job convincing him that I was worthy and that I could make something of myself. She just did not do as good of a job convincing me. The patterns of low self-worth were set in stone. I did go to college, my Dad did pay for two full years, then I dropped out, came home and got married. I fulfilled his expectations…

My first roommate was a Senior on academic probation who was required to move back into the dorm. I was locked out of my room on a regular basis. She was partying with groups of guys and various drugs and alcohol. I was a goody goody and would not think of participating and was not invited anyway. I often spent the night in the common area/floor lounge. My second roommate was a freshman who was intrigued by sex. She plastered our walls with Playgirl nudes and brought men to our dorm room on a regular basis which again, sent me to the common area to sleep. About this time, I met my husband to be. He was three years older than me, a fraternity guy, and a party animal when it came to alcohol and drugs (as was quite common in those mid 70's college times) I was in love, going to "fix" him and going to be the girl of his dreams.

I was still wondering in my late Sophomore year, what I was going to "be". I had changed majors 4 times, searching for a degree that did not require math skills because I had been told so many times that I was bad at Math. I believed them all. At this time my guy, who a short time later became my husband, came to me and said "Well, its been fun but I am graduating and going back to my hometown". I responded that I was ready to quit school, come home and would work to save some money for "our" future. My summer job became a full-time clerical job where I saved money to get married less than 2 years later. We had a perfect plan, a wedding, an apartment and two decent jobs. 4 weeks before the wedding, his company closed, and he was unemployed. In an interesting turn of events, he found a job one state away! The day after the wedding, we strapped a mattress to the roof of our sedan, tossed in 20 or so boxes of wedding presents and drove to our new apartment that was leased with a telephone call. (no video walkthroughs or internet showings back then of course). It turned out OK. Apartment was good, his job was good, we met great people who took us under their wing, we went on a couple of nice vacations, I tried out a couple of different jobs and we tried for kids. Unfortunately, only one of us was trying. He was too busy with the "guys" playing golf, tennis, racquetball, bowling, out for drinks. I spent many nights home alone or working at my retail store job.

I made the most of my jobs and actually loved the retail life. Strangely, I always seemed to fall back into the pattern of being targeted by a bully, someone I worked with that saw my insecurities and took advantage of me. It happened over and over, position and location after location. I was often sad and alone. 7 years after moving to this new state, I started looking into outside sales positions. I was always the last choice because of having no experience and no college degree. Finally, I received a job offer with a company where the hiring manager said, "I'm probably making the worst decision of my life, but we are going to give you a try". That instilled little confidence! I did end up being fairly successful to his surprise until the company was sold, and they no longer needed a sales rep in my territory. I then moved into a sales position with a well-known company and built a level of success that surprised everyone.

About this time, my husband started feeling intimidated by my level of success. I was not allowed to talk about my success. I had married someone just like me with very fragile insecurities. He decided he was not happy with his rise up the ladder at his inside sales position and decided to move to a 100% commission sales position with an investment company. We discussed it and decided it was the perfect time to try it because I was doing ok financially, and we didn't have/couldn't have kids. I was almost 30 (which was incredibly old to start having kids at that time) and he was 33. The week after he quit his job and gave up his salary and benefits, I learned I was pregnant! I was deliriously happy to be pregnant, continued to work up until the day my son was born and was receiving calls from clients the day I came home from the hospital. I took care of my son, worked long hours, seldom slept and supported us while he "got his business up and running".

"THE PERFECT FAMILY"

This never happened. His insecurities and lack of self-esteem kept him from building his clientele. It kept him from selling anything that would earn commissions. In addition, he worked for an Extreme Bully. This Bully he worked for taught him how to bully me. It was very subtle, but I was not allowed to show my success. I was not allowed to talk about what went on in my work world. I could cook and clean and play Susie homemaker and he could pretend that the money that came in the household magically appeared. To admit that it came from me and my hard work would be admitting that he was a failure.....so I played the charade to protect his self-esteem. This set up the silent anger that stayed with us for the next 20 years. Everyone said I was so lucky! I was married to the nicest guy ever, the guy that would give you the shirt off his back. At home however, my job was to keep the anger at a simmer. Four years after my son, my daughter came along, the perfect family. 4 days after my son was born, he wiped out my personal savings account by lying to the bank teller. That was the first of many times he stole money from me, the kids, our investment accounts and others to save face.

The Extreme Bully at the investment firm decided that

my husband was not cut out for the job and set him up to ruin his reputation. The state said he could not sell investments anymore and he proceeded to roll from unemployed to short-term job to unemployed and on and on. He did not apply for State unemployment benefits because that perfect job was always right around the corner. I often wonder if I had been stronger, put my foot down, yelled, screamed, said the painful things, if I had given the ultimate ultimatum, would he have gone a different route. The route he took was down, way down. He had always had a strong interest in porn which became what he turned to for the last 20 years of our 30 year marriage. I knew it was there and I knew it was somewhat normal for men to have an interest, but it was extreme. Later, it explained the rejection I experienced. I thought it was so cool that we were the first of all of our friends with internet and PCs. I learned eventually it was mainly for his Porn habit. He had always liked card games and board games and he was extremely competitive which turned into gambling. Gambling in order to replace the income I expected in a weekly paycheck that never came. In the early 2000s, credit card companies would send out letters saying, "your pre-approved". All you had to do is go online and accept. As I was earning a little money, I was getting the offers and he was accepting them without my knowledge. He also opened a PO box and had all the bills go to that address so that I never knew what he was doing. There was a storm brewing and things were starting to blow up.

Pornography was taking up much of his time and when there wasn't money coming in, he decided to make it up with gambling. I learned eventually that he was spending every day, 8 till 8 or 9 pm at the Casino playing video poker. He was actually pretty successful (he thought). At one point, when I learned about all of the credit card debt and that it was from gambling and paying credit card bills with other credit cards. I asked him how he could do this to his family. His answer was, what is the big deal, I made $25,000 this year. I said OK, how much did you lose? He had no idea. In addition to the Porn and the gambling, strangely enough, he became addicted to our church. He was there every Sunday, serving as usher, elder, evangelizing in neighborhoods and sharing God with anyone who would listen. Eventually, the counselor he was seeing at my request, said he had to quit the church as it was allowing him to "Do Good" in order to justify all the evil he was involved in.

Little things had happened earlier in the marriage, but my mom had always said, if the marriage doesn't work, it's your fault, fix it. My parents even joked that they loved him so much, if the marriage didn't work, they would take him over me. I decided that I could fix him and if I couldn't, then I was the failure. Lots of steps to marriage failure with all these patterns repeating in our lives.

How much of what he became was because I allowed him to become this person in our relationship? How much of what I allowed was because I had a pattern of allowing people to take advantage due to my lack of self-worth? These questions will never be answered. I have forgiven him for all the lies and the financial ruin, all the deceit. I take responsibility for "allowing the behavior" and being whiney and complaining to my friends but never doing anything about it. A strong Christian friend of mine suggested I end the marriage. I told her I wasn't ready because I just didn't want to be alone. She said, "Nancy, you are already more alone than anyone I have ever known".

The tail end of this part of the story is, I filed for divorce after he told me I should. I said, "how can I go day to day and trust you with all your lies?" and he said, get a lawyer. I did the next day. When I handed him the paperwork he said "What?? I told you to get a lawyer to protect your money, not to divorce me". (He was referring to my inheritance from my dad that we were living on but he had no access to) It was already done, and I went forward with it. 6 months later, on our 30-year wedding anniversary, the divorce was final. He fought the idea for a little while and then ran full speed ahead with online dating, plenty of women and generally making my life and my future look bleak. There were loads of debt, an upside-down house value from all the times we refinanced to pay off bills and now I was alone. I had no alimony and all the debt because the divorce attorney was supposedly protecting my credit, as if that was the most important thing. I was to receive $3,000 a month to pay a $7,000 a month minimum credit card payment plus I would get a little child support. The attorney said no worries, if he doesn't pay, we will just put him in jail. The divorce attorney took advantage of me as well.

The crazy punch line of this part of the story is, 9 weeks later, a Medical Examiner and a Police officer knocked on my door at 10pm on a Thursday night to inform me that he had died of a Heart Attack (at 53 years old) I really did not want him out of my life that way! I was heartbroken and devastated to lose my partner of 30 years. I had not only his betrayal in so many areas of life, but also his leaving me in a complete state of mental and financial devastation. I even took responsibility for the funeral for my kid's sake. Some of the people around me asked if I was happy that he was dead. My daughter, who was then 16, asked if I was happy that he was gone. I was not happy he was gone. I was not happy with the financial mess I was in. I had no idea where my life was going or where I would end up.

LIFE: PART 2

There is a part 2 in my life. At 51 years old everything had changed drastically. All along the way, my faith was with me. I was not one to say why me, it was more a matter of why now. What should I do? How will I survive this? Deep down I knew I would survive but not how the story would end. It was just an inner voice telling me it would all be ok.

Where did I end up? Well, I had to let my house go to foreclosure because it had been refinanced multiple times before the divorce to roll in some of the gambling and credit debt. It was very upside down, value to debt. I filed bankruptcy after negotiating and paying off most of the debt. My wonderful territory sales position that I loved suddenly "downsized" and I was unemployed and my daughter was heading off to college soon (my son was already in college). Both of my parents and my wonderful dog had passed away 3 years earlier.

When you think of identities, I had lost all of mine. I was no longer a mom, a wife, a homeowner or an employee. I was not a daughter, a pet Mom, a caregiver. I had lost them all. I was feeling completely alone and helpless....

Was I devastated? Was I confused? Was I disoriented? Heck Yeah...

My daughter was 17 and planning her escape to college and our relationship was very strained. I had kept her father's "issues" out of the forefront for years, in fact, she thought we had a perfect family. Loving Mom and Dad, hard working Mom, nice house in the suburbs. The year before I filed for divorce, we looked normal. Suddenly for her, that all fell apart. Our communication was strained and everything I did or did not do was another disappointment to her.

My husband had started online dating months BEFORE I filed for divorce, and I started talking to men on dating websites soon after the divorce was final. I became obsessed with online communication games and slowly began dating. I thought my husband was the worst through most of the previous 20 years and then I learned, there were many men in the sea with many of the same problems. I could write a book about all the dates I had between October and July. I started to forgive my husband during this time. I also learned that I had to forgive myself.

I realized that I HAD THE POWER TO PUT MY FOOT DOWN earlier in our marriage when I saw things going bad. I realized how many times I yelled and complained about his predilections and was not consistent with boundaries. Yes, to coin a term, I was a classic enabler. I allowed his behavior to go on and on and I continued to believe I would be able to "fix" him or maybe this treatment was all I deserved. This realization of my own power was a start to "breaking the pattern". I learned at this time about Narcissistic behavior and realized that my husband had slowly adapted into one. Or he was one all along and I allowed the personality traits to come out. A Narcissist must have someone to blame for everything. I was that person. I referred earlier to his addiction to pornography. I did not know how intense his addiction was, but I see now that it started to infiltrate our marriage immediately 30 years before. He was not interested in sex with me and there was always a reason. And I always accepted the reason and the blame. For almost 30 years I believed I was fat and stupid and could not possibly survive without a man like him. I wore socks to bed, or I took baths, or I read books at night and all of these things were "turn offs" for him. And, like when my mother told me I was fat and "not very smart", I believed them. The gym teacher also blamed me, and I accepted the blame. This realization is when I began to believe I could break the pattern. Dating in this 10-month time period opened my eyes to so many things. I was not unattractive, I was not thin, but I was not grotesque, and I could manage my life without a man permanently taking care of me. I told every one of these men I dated that I did not want a permanent relationship. I just wanted to enjoy life for a while!

With the loss of all my other identities, I was

wondering what in the world I was going to do with my life. About this time an old friend reminded me I had always wanted to go back and finish my college education that had been cut short to get married. I decided I WOULD DO IT! I started college in the Fall of 2009 with 43 credits from the 1970s. (they were very generous with those credits and a scholarship). I went to school full-time for three years and graduated in May of 2012 with a degree in Communication. This gave me so much self-worth, taught me I could DO it, and allowed me to connect with so many women of so many diverse backgrounds. I gained so much in those three years! I learned to be proud of myself!

Early 2009 I met my forever guy. Very soon we found that the "troubles" we had each experienced in our lives, divorce, foreclosure, bankruptcy…. they were not who we were, they were what made each of us stronger and better. We helped each other recover from those experiences and we build each other up instead of tearing each other down. We each have grown-up kids that call each other "the sibs" and some are good friends. I personally have pledged that I will never get married again. We are in a committed relationship; we depend on each other and know each other inside and out but do not feel a ceremony and a ring make the difference. Who we are and how we support each other is what is important. Does my Catholic upbringing make me feel a tiny bit of guilt sometimes because of "Living in Sin"? Yes, but It feels right.

While going to school, I worked two or three part-time jobs and simply had faith it would all work out. There was God and my faith again, giving me comfort that it would all work out. Upon graduation, I started the "career" job search where I was always the second choice for a job. I was trained, I had skills, I had experience from my past life but…. I was 56 years old. Maybe the employers felt I would not be in it for the long haul. I took an unpaid internship as a last resort in order to have something to put on my resume for future job applications. I worked for a national nonprofit organization and helped them with their volunteer program. After 3 months I was "promoted" to a paid employee, working with major companies, speaking and encouraging their employees to make payroll contributions to the organization. Those contributions were then distributed to individual nonprofit organizations. I met with the executive directors of those organizations who would be getting the donations on a regular basis and connected to one particular woman. She liked my age, my maturity, my new college skills and asked me to come work for her at her nonprofit. I felt I was on my way to being appreciated and valued and I was going to have an impact on people who needed me! I was very wrong. After all, I had been through, I met the one woman who could take away everything I had gained. This woman thrived on controlling people. She was truly a Jekyll and Hyde personality. She could be so sweet one moment and a monster the next. I found myself at my desk at 9am, crying by 10am. She was so difficult, it was a barrier to my being able to help the clients we served. I was still interviewing, still being 2nd choice over and over and horribly miserable. How could I go through so much in my life over the last many years and end up here? One day I answered the phone to a woman asking if I was still looking for a job. She asked me if I would like to sell government products to Seniors. I said, "That's Insurance, no possible way!" She said your problem is that you need more interviewing experience. I said I had plenty of interviewing experience, I just needed "hiring" experience. She convinced me to go to the interview for the learning value. I told her that I had always said I would not sell insurance "over my dead body". What could be more boring, confusing and lack reward?

As you might have guessed, I went to the interview and was hired. I spent the next 4 months every evening, studying at home online. (Thank you, college experience, for giving me the ability to do it). I finally passed the State Life and Health Exam and was able to go into my "crazy lady boss" and resign. It took me 11 months to get away from her. My new career was 100% commission. If I had not experienced the misery of working with this "crazy" woman, I never would have had the courage or confidence to take a 100% commission job. I went into it with total confidence that I could do it and make enough to support myself. Little did I know, a new woman would be my trainer and boss. This woman, a few years younger than I was, had a huge level of success and did not want to have to train me, but would make a commission off of my sales. She too treated me like dirt. Was I asking for it? Did people detect the ability to abuse me? Was it like a perfume I gave off? Abuse Nancy and feel better about yourself? Whatever it was, she belittled me one time too many. After screaming at me, in front of a room full of other agents (all men), that I was F-ing stupid, I walked out of the door into the insurance office down the road which happened to be my current company. I took this woman's verbal abuse for 4 months and never again.

In that insurance company office down the road, I found the career, the mentoring, the success that I never could have dreamed of. After years of drought, I found the waterfall. I have a sense of financial security that I never experienced in my entire life and never dreamed I would have. I work very, very hard and am rewarded by the people who tell me they couldn't have navigated their Medicare and their personal safety without me. I receive clients 100% through networking and referrals and I am continually surprised by the people who call me and say "I was told you are the only one to work with because you know what you're talking about" As I age, it gets easier and easier to hear these compliments and to accept them.

In 2014, I met the "Personal Coach" I mentioned in my first paragraph. She is the one that helped me see that I had been controlled and abused by a multitude of individuals through my life. She saw the pattern and congratulated me because the abuse that lasted years, verbal or sexual, with my Mom, the gym teacher and my Husband had evolved into the same type of treatment at many turns. My last "move" took only 4 months to see and to act on. I HAD BROKEN THE PATTERN. I have learned to spot that pattern and to move on. When I feel the same thing happening, I put a stop to it. I have had to walk away from long time friendships as well as acquaintances that look like they may turn into controlling situations. I have become a new person. I now have faith in myself, my "smarts", my abilities, my knowing the "right" thing to do for my clients. I trust my decisions, my actions, my thoughts. I have developed a reputation for helping people for the correct reason. I do not look at how things will benefit me but how they will benefit them, and my success has grown. The most important factor is that I learned that I am ENOUGH. God loves me and is there for me. I am not lacking or less than anyone else. I am smart and kind and successful and have people who love me and care for me for who I am.

I have broken the pattern. I hope you can too!

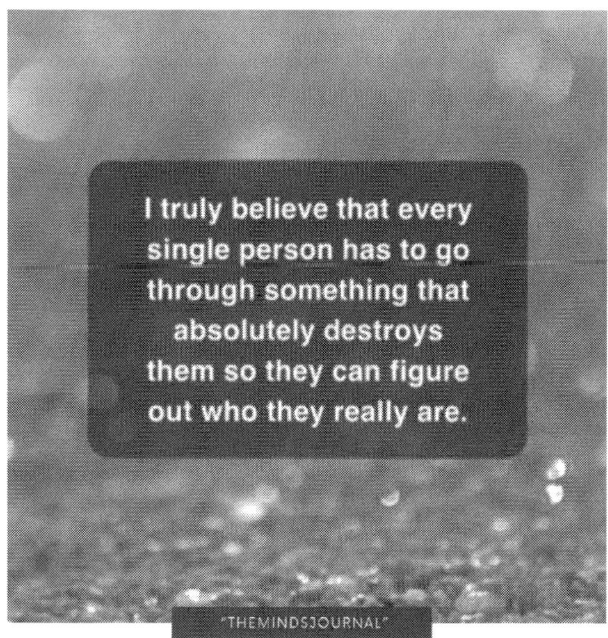

"TheMindsJournal"

ACKNOWLEDGMENTS

I would like to Thank CK, the man I always dreamed of, my Knight in Shining Armour, who puts up with my nonstop hours, helping my clients! I would also like to thank all of the people who have challenged me in my life, some of whom are described in this chapter. They have made me the NEW, improved person that I am.

ABOUT AUTHOR

I have always been a voracious reader and thought I would someday write a book. I didn't know what it would be about because certainly, no one would want to hear about my crazy life! It would be too sad and depressing. Then, my life turned around and has had a happy re-beginning. Then, Dorris came along and allowed me to tell my story in a chapter. Who knows, it may extend to a full book someday!

ABOUT MY BUSINESS

I am a Health Insurance Broker with a large company located all over the US. I am able to help all ages, protect themselves, Head to Toe, from catastrophic medical costs that could occur. I concentrate on the Medicare side, helping people navigate the complexities of how to sign up, when to sign up, and what you need to add to it for protection. I am licensed in Wisconsin only and love every minute of what I do!

Facebook Personal Page
Nancy Towle (Nancy Blameuser Towle)

Instagram
NTowle50

THANK YOU!

If you are having trouble with RX costs, send me an email and I will reply with a list of organizations that you can contact that MAY help you. I spend a great deal of time with my clients helping them hold down their drug costs and this may help! If you live in Wisconsin, please call me to help with your Health Insurance, Life, Cancer, Heart/Stroke, Dental and Vision needs!

Tiffaney Whipple

MY FRIEND SATURN

This story is about my friend Saturn and how she helped me to mature and embrace who I am. She will be introduced a little later in the story, but let me begin by sharing about who I am and what I do. I am an educator, entrepreneur, wife and mother. And, I think it is also important to share that I am an astrologer and love to talk and learn about all the "woo-woo" kinds of things. I believe we should all do our best at being who we desire to be and not making excuses for our decisions whether they turned out as we wished or not. Don't think I have that fully together yet; I am still a work in progress. Just this past week I had one of my "emotional" breakdowns that I was not able to control. While growing up, I figured out how to suppress all of the emotional baggage and get distracted by something else, like work, school, marriage or my children. At this stage in my life, that no longer works. I now understand what is happening when these extreme emotional periods occur. I've been doing the inner work and listening to what my soul & spirit guides are telling me. Five years ago, I didn't feel comfortable telling my story. I was concerned about being judged and rejected. Part of my work is getting past all of that and understanding what I am truly here to do in this lifetime.

Sometimes we do things for others. That is not a bad thing, unless it truly does not honor what we really want. As a child, I always saw myself moving away and exploring life in a different way. I grew up in a small town, Louisville, Kentucky, home of The Kentucky Derby (horse racing), Muhammad Ali, and let's not forget the Louisville Slugger. Yet, I wanted to know how the rest of the world lived. I wanted to have different experiences that would be considered outside of the norm for my family, like astrology, tarot cards, psychic experiences and more. I danced to the beat of my own drum. I was a risk-taker and often found myself in trouble. I grew up being on a "punishment" for the majority of my teenage years because I just had to do what I wanted to do. I was the one who was told to be in by midnight and showed up at 3:00 in the morning, fully aware that there were consequences. I would do this because the excitement of where I was and what I was doing was worth the trouble I would be in when I arrived home.

As I matured, I evolved into someone who realized that I was no longer embracing that adventurous teenager that lived within. At times she would rear her beautiful head and I was back at it. Yet, with the responsibilities of life, such as marriage, motherhood & my career, I would quietly put her back in the box and do the things I was "supposed to do". So I joined churches and other organizations to belong to a group, but it was rare that I felt complete. What the F*@$! I remember sitting one day and thinking to myself, "This is not how my life is supposed to be". Doing what society thinks I should do and be. Unbeknownst to me, Saturn was really making an impression on my life. We were acquaintances but I wasn't really calling her my friend just yet. I wanted to ignore her and for her to leave me alone. I had not yet realized that she has always been there and will always be.

In astrology, my friend Saturn is the planet of hard work and responsibility. She is the influence in our lives that disciplines us until we discipline ourselves. She teaches us the lessons we must learn in this lifetime. You may not be friends with her, but you definitely know her. Though she is more like a stern parent rather than a friend, I choose to call her friend because the influence she has on my life is beneficial to my growth as a person. Every seven years or so, she will drop in to check if I am doing my life's work. Some visits are more significant than others, yet they are all important milestones in my life. She shows up with the power to push me forward to evolve. My friend Saturn is a water sign and she comes periodically to remind me to do my emotional work; which I avoided for years. Some of her visits have included divorce, changes in family dynamics, and relationship issues. These are the things that required me to face the music and deal with the emotions I dreaded dealing with.

I HAD TO CHOOSE MYSELF

At age 20, Saturn was on her way to visit me. This of course wasn't the first time and we were not friends yet. I was away at Kentucky State University, in my junior year of college and had just found out I was pregnant. I had no idea what life would now be like. I wasn't married and wasn't sure I ever wanted to get married. But after sitting out at the end of the fall semester of college, I realized it was time to get serious and grow up. Fast forward some 4-5 years, I was married, had a son and a daughter and had just bought a house. I was happy some of the time, but not always. I stayed in the marriage because I thought it was what I was supposed to do. As years went by, I realized it wasn't getting better and I had to make a change. I knew a lot of people would be upset, but I had to choose myself in that situation and so I left and never looked back.

By the time I left my husband, I had already had religious and spiritual experiences that helped to shape and mold who I was. And unbeknownst to me, I had a lot more to go. Let me explain further. I wasn't raised in a religious or spiritual household, though my parents were raised as Christians. In our house, Sundays were for cleaning, not going to church; unless it was Easter or Mother's Day. One particular Mother's Day Sunday, after the shouting, singing, and the long-winded sermon, the pastor began his closing and he then asked, is there one? He began walking down the steps from the pulpit, stretching out his right hand and using a handkerchief to wipe his sweaty brow with his left. He was still preaching and then he asked again, is there one? By this time, I am almost in a trance. I was unsure of what was happening to me. I had never felt this before. It was as if someone or something had taken over my body. And by the time he asked, is there one? again, I was pushing people out of my way so I could go and grab his hand. When I grabbed his hand, the entire congregation began making noise and celebrating. After everything returned to what I'd call normal, my family had a shocked look on their face. I couldn't explain it. But I was not joking. I remember an intense feeling of love that caused me to cry. It was the first time in this lifetime that I felt such love and also the beginning of more spiritual experiences that would follow.

I have always been intrigued by all things "woo-woo"; especially astrology and dreams. I studied astrology over the years and in my studies, I mostly focused on figuring myself out. Damn, what a complex creature I am. And actually, we all are. One thing I learned is about my dreams. The way my friend Saturn affects my astrological birth chart is significant to my dream life. I am what is considered a Saturian and as a Saturian, I have very vivid dreams that involve this lifetime, as well as past lifetimes. It has been this way my entire life. My dreams range from prophetic dreams to warning dreams to symbolic dreams; where I have to wake up and interpret the meaning. Some dreams tell me to reach out to someone and deliver a message. The *"message delivery"* kind of dreams were the ones that used to scare me the most, because I lacked confidence in myself. I feared sharing the information would make no sense to the intended party. In my adult life, I began getting past-life dreams that remind me of the work I came to do in *this* lifetime. Some do not believe that we have all lived many different lifetimes, yet I do. My friend Saturn helped to make this all real for me.

Once, with the help of a past life regression therapist,

I remembered another lifetime I once lived. I was a young woman in an unloving marriage, a mother to a young daughter and a wife to an abusive husband. I felt hopelessly stuck in my situation and very unhappy. The abuse didn't stop with the husband, even his family mistreated me and left me out. I had nowhere to go, and for whatever reason, my parents would not allow me to come stay with them. I was treated as if I wasn't there and I definitely didn't have a voice in the marriage. One day my husband was tired of me being around and flat out told me to leave. He didn't like nor love me. However, he did love our daughter and did not consider us to be a package deal. The daughter was staying, and he was not up for negotiations. This was apparently a time before joint custody and shared parenting. What the man of the house said was law. I remember the strong emotional feelings of despair, distraught & agony. My Daughter! The only person on this earth who loved me back! I begged to stay and promised to be better-whatever that meant-yet my husband said no. He told me I would never see my daughter again and to never come back.

Broken and aimlessly wandering, I stumbled across a small house that sat on a river. The owner was an older Indian woman with a long braid down her back. She lived in this small house with her adult son and daughter. They took me into their home and treated me as family. The older woman took care of me when I felt there was nothing to keep living for. This feeling was the intense love I had never felt before. Me and the Indian woman became really close and had an unbreakable bond. The older woman was like the mother I never had; she taught me so much in our time together. We spent many years together and that sealed our bond to last over many lifetimes. When the older lady was on her deathbed, I stayed by her side, along with her children, until she took her last breath. I still remember the intense emotion and sadness due to the loss of someone so loved. That was a past life regression I did roughly 10 years ago and I recognized the soul of the older woman and who she is in this lifetime. I was also able to recognize the souls of her children. It is all quite amazing how the past life works and how you can recognize souls though they look different from lifetime to lifetime.

Honestly, I still have karmic issues related to that lifetime. The way I entered relationships in this lifetime, and how I behaved while in them, all made more sense after the past life regression session. Whenever a relationship became too aggressive or I felt mistreated, I would end it and walk away. However the negative side to that karmic energy is that I did not open up and trust very easily, most likely letting various opportunities pass me by. The past life regression of this woman and her children helped me to recognize this. Who was this woman and her children? This woman entered into my current lifetime when I was 28 years of age as my youngest child and she is a blessing I am so grateful for. She came along when another relationship was going bad, my first marriage. She came back to remind me of my strength and that I am truly loved. Her adult children in the past life are now her older siblings in this lifetime. She took care of me in that lifetime when I was broken and now, I take care of her and her kids in this lifetime. I was amazed when I discovered this rich soul history. From birth, my youngest daughter was very attached to me. It wasn't so much the same with my older two children. Of course they love me and I love them; however, those two have their own special karmic relationship with one another. When my youngest daughter was very young, she loved to be around me so much that it was common for me to wake up in the morning and find that she had jumped out of her crib and crawled into my bed. She loved being around me. We were connected on a deeper level, and her soul was trying to remind me of that bond. Sounds crazy? Well, I am just getting started. Let me tell you more about when my friend Saturn visited.

STARTING OVER

One of the lessons my friend Saturn reminds me of when she visits is that I came into this life to learn about family, the home and handling my emotions. For most of my life, I ignored, denied, & suppressed my emotions. After all, I was nurtured that way. I am a very sensitive person but only those close to me know that. I don't have close ties to family like I would like, other than the closeness I share with my children. I grew up in a home that wasn't very touchy feely; not emotionally or physically. When I cried, which wasn't often, I was encouraged to suck it up and keep it moving. It wasn't until I got older that I realized physical love and verbal affection was something I silently longed for.

By 2004, during a Saturn visit, I was a single mother with 3 young children aged, 7, 5, and 1 year old. My son is the oldest and I have 2 daughters. I was teaching middle school science at an alternative high school during the day and working on my master's degree in school counseling by night. There was rent, weekly daycare bill, and a whole lot of other bills that I was now ultimately responsible for. My ex-husband and I owned the home I moved out of and it was pending foreclosure. I remember the mixed emotions I was feeling at the time. I felt free (from being in a relationship), anxious about how I was going to pay all the bills and scared shitless because I had 3 little ones whose lives were in my hands. I ultimately felt the pressure. I still remember a few nights after I moved into the 3 bedroom apartment in the suburbian area of Louisville. I had put the kids to bed and I sat in my bathtub and cried. I believe I cried because I was scared but I also believe some of the tears were mourning the ended relationship and looking at "starting over". The inner voice within, my soul, was reminding me that I chose and needed this. It wasn't an overnight decision to leave the marriage. I had time to think, pray, sleep on it, seek wise counsel, think again, pray again, and so on and so forth. So when the decision was made, I was clear and I knew it was best for me to leave the relationship and never look back. We had outgrown one another. I didn't hate him or wish anything bad for him, I just wanted to be free. We had been married for 7 years at that time, so we gave it a good shot. So why was I crying? Because no matter how much I wanted out of that situation, I had no clue of what lay ahead of me. I didn't have a solid plan past getting out. So I was there…..and now what?

In 2010 Saturn cycled around for another visit. By this time, I was remarried and also helping to raise 2 stepchildren. My new husband and I had moved from

Louisville to New Jersey in 2007 and then we bought a home in Cheltenham, Pennsylvania in 2010. My stepchildren came to live with us about a year prior to our move to Pennsylvania. I will never forget how excited I was. It was Christmas eve and my husband had gone to pick them up and bring them to live with us in our tiny 3 bedroom apartment in New Jersey. I remember thinking how great it was going to be to have 5 children in the home and I didn't have to do labor and delivery again. My children were excited too. My son was looking forward to having a little brother. That didn't last too long. The children were fine at first and then shit changed. I felt at odds with my stepchildren and could not grasp why there was so much trouble with blending the family. I asked for my husband's assistance because after all, he was their biological parent. That did not work too well. He was going through his own adjustment period to being their full-time caregiver. The tension and lack of connection with them really weighed on me. I couldn't understand how I could go to work everyday and build a family environment in my classroom with students who came from different neighborhoods and walks of life, but couldn't manage to do it in my own home. I took it really personally and knowing what I know now, I shouldn't have.

By the time we moved into our home in Pennsylvania, I was working on my doctorate degree in school leadership, working a full-time job as a project based learning teacher, helping to raise 5 children and losing my mind. I ended up opting to get a second master's degree in school leadership which eased some of my burden but then tension arose amongst the kids. Eventually, it got to the point where my husband and his children moved to an apartment in New York (because he was working there at the time) and I stayed here in Pennsylvania with my kids. We continued our relationship because we still loved each other dearly. His children stayed with him in New York for a year or so and then they went back to live with their mother. To this day, I do not have a relationship with my stepchildren. There are no phone calls or happy birthday text messages. It just is what it is. Whenever we are all in the same place, only one of them will give me a dry "hello" and that is only if their mother is not present. I wish it didn't have to be this way but that is out of my control. I used to say that I tried my best when they were here living with us, but in retrospect, I did not do all that I could have. Like they say, hindsight is 20/20.

I do not blame them for their behavior. I believe we all come into lifetimes for different reasons and purposes. The stepchildren had to show me myself and they did a damn good job. They helped to bring up things from both this lifetime and past lifetimes, like feeling rejected and left out. No matter how old you are, or how well you can disguise it, that shit hurts. I have gotten to a point spiritually, where I can see beyond the human behaviors and find the reminders and lessons in the situation. Don't mistake this as me saying I allow disrespect directed towards me; yet, I can ignore being ignored. It is like my father said when I was a child, "Not everyone is going to like you, baby girl. So What!" My friend Saturn comes around without hesitation to remind me to do my emotional and family work. I have hit some home runs in this lifetime and I have also struck out. But I am still here.

Saturn visited me last in 2019, the year I quit my 20 year career as an educator and became a full-fledged entrepreneur. That was a scary and exciting time. Since then, I have started my business as an astrologer. I incorporate my experience as an educator with my knowledge of astrology to create courses and live webinars, and provide various types of astrological readings. I focus on the astrological aspects that help people both in their professional and personal lives. My friend Saturn helped me to have the courage to do this and now, through my astrology practice, I introduce her to other people so they can become friends with her too. I am able to let others know when she is planning to visit, how long she will stay and what area of life she would like to focus on, so they can prepare for her. She is quite intriguing. I have not always appreciated my friend Saturn, but I most definitely do now. She and I will spend time together again in May 2026 and I will be ready to see my old friend. After all, she refuses to stop visiting.

ACKNOWLEDGMENTS

Writing this chapter has been a great experience. I would like to first thank my parents, Phillip Montgomery Jr. and Alexis Montgomery for giving me life. They taught me to be honest and not worry so much about what people think about me. They showed me how to be strong and to handle challenges in my life and keep moving forward. I owe them everything for choosing to raise me with confidence and the belief that all things are possible if you focus your mind. I want to thank my husband of 15 years, Vincent Whipple for always supporting me in my endeavors; no matter how crazy some of them have been. He knows how to counsel me when I am a little unsure and definitely assists me with words when mine are a little too blunt. Vincent has changed my life in so many ways and that includes various exposures to the finer things in life. I am grateful that he and I both chose to come back in this lifetime and share it together. Our love is one that transcends lifetimes. It is a soul connection. I want to thank my children, Emon, Melia, and Nila Anthony. They too have changed my life in so many ways. Emon showed me how to grow up and be a mother, Melia taught me how to be more caring to others, and Nila showed me how to turn dreams into reality. I am so proud of the young adults they have become and I look forward to the next chapters in their lives. I love the closeness of our relationships because collectively they give me the love and connection that My Friend Saturn in Cancer makes me yearn for. Finally to all the others who influenced my life in significant ways: My grandfather, Phillip Montgomery Sr., My Grandmothers, Albertha Higgs and Rose Marie Montgomery (RIP), My Aunt, Senator Georgia Powers (RIP), My Uncle Glenn Thomas Montgomery (RIP), My brother, Phillip Montgomery III, My best friend, Tiffany Kelly Hill, My Soul Sister, Tenia Thompson, and My Spring 1994 DEEPCOVER Line Sisters from The Alpha Pi Chapter of Delta Sigma Theta Sorority Incorporated.

ABOUT AUTHOR

Tiffaney Joy, also known as Astral Joy, has studied astrology for many years and recently decided to share her gift of astrological insights with the world. Her astrology readings span basic astrology, exploring your soul purpose and synastry (comparing charts of two or more people for compatibility). Tiffaney has been a public school educator for over 20 years and enjoys teaching about astrology and leadership. Her educational background includes two Master's Degrees, one in School Leadership and another in School Counseling & Personnel Services. She also holds a Bachelors in Biological Sciences, has extended graduate studies in Curriculum and Instructional Design, and a leadership certification in coaching, speaking, and training from the internationally recognized John C. Maxwell Group. She created Astral Joy to help individuals gain insight about themselves, whether it pertains to their personal life, love life, career, family and more. We all can harness the power and energies from God, the universe, and our guardian angels and Astral Joy will show you how. Do you want to understand yourself, your partner, or family members better in order to improve your relationships? Get an astrological reading that will provide you with spiritual insight and assist in all areas of your life.

ABOUT MY BUSINESS

Astral Joy Astrology was created to help people get more in touch with who they are on a deeper soul level. There are basic astrology readings, synastry readings, and soul purpose readings.

Website
https://www.astraljoy.com/

Facebook Personal Page
https://www.facebook.com/tiffaneywhipple1/

Instagram
https://www.instagram.com/astral_joy/

THANK YOU!

My Free Course, Who I Am Astrology. https://astral-joy.newzenler.com/courses/who-i-am-astrology-workshop

Brianne DiDino

LIFE EXPERIENCES BRING THE GREATEST GUIDANCE

Before you begin, please take a minute to grab your favorite drink, take a couple of deep breaths and then continue into this chapter. Certain parts of this story may catch everyone's eye and heart a little differently. So, allow yourself to embrace the precious time needed to connect and feel what arises within you as you read. This is truly the key to understanding what I'm about to discuss. Here we go!

With so many emotions to explore, some of the scariest aspects of being alive is experiencing the feelings of being broken and/or hopeless. When we possess limited confidence and self-value, a sense of confusion in what to do appears when overcoming these mindsets. Some may have difficulty in seeing anything inspiring to help nudge them forward in their next steps. Please consider that these arising mindsets and emotions are not in vain. They are as important as a beacon in the night to your own self-discovery. They contain the clues to what your Soul is longing to understand within its precious time here. The beautiful silver lining is that we already possess the most enlightening and precious gift of guidance. Our very own

Life's Story is a seriously overlooked asset by which we can **review** our experiences and feelings, find positive value within our **lessons learned**, **adjust** our perspectives, and then **move** forward into a more beneficial direction. We will continue this learning curve while here until our Soul becomes fulfilled in everything that it wishes to gain wisdom on.

In the short decades of my life thus far, I've been blessed in having several "Eureka!" moments of which I'm excited to share. Through my own Story and what it has highlighted for me, was the ability to see my genuine self and purpose. Hopefully, my gained insights can spark a little intrigue into yours so that every step you take brings even more understanding, love, confidence, peace and joy your way.

I am a firm believer that the Universe and our time here gives us enough information to navigate through life. The simplest thing can actually be one of the greatest clues and connections to our purpose. Here's a curious question for you, "Has there ever been a childhood movie or anything else that has simply captivated your attention?" Becoming even more awestruck as you watch how every struggle that the main character seemed to have had was completely healed by a whole-hearted decision. If it happens to be a song or anything else that pulls you in, where do your memories and feelings take you?

Hands down, my significant connection is with the 1982 movie "Annie" by John Huston. When this movie comes on, I quickly settle in and get so wrapped up in watching Annie, it's as if I transform into her. It's so easy to become glued to how courageous, strong and secure she is in this story. What's even more mesmerizing is that she always seems to know what she wants in life even when her circumstances are so bleak. I longed to understand what that little, red-headed girl had passionately and innately seemed to know about the powerful topics of trust and love. It didn't dawn on me until later on in life that this exact movie highlighted tons of aspects by which my own Soul wanted more guidance. The majority of us never realize how truly intuitive we are and that we already possess the knowledge and guidance that we need. As I said before, our Life's Story is our roadmap to which we can **review**, find value within our **lessons**, **adjust** our perspectives and **move** into a more beneficial direction to which our powerful free-will can take us. So, here is my own personal example of how I utilized this learning curve as a guidance system. As long as I can remember, I've been filled with many thoughts, feelings and questions such as: "not being good enough, I don't belong here, I'm always misunderstood, I don't fit in, soft is for the weak, I'm TOO MUCH, and What's trust and love…is either real?" More than half the battle is grasping an understanding of what happened that caused your self-protection mode to engage. Once you begin to know the pivotal and even the minor events, you can then work on healing and consciously making more loving decisions for your authentic self.

After many review-sessions of my story, several influential catalysts helped bring to light my overly self-guarded persona. A huge factor of my foundation leads back to acknowledging that my dad was an extremely tough alcoholic in my younger years. He was taught the core value system of using negative reinforcement. Also, he would abuse my mom on a physical, mental and emotional level, and was quite the unfaithful, antisocial recluse who preferred us to be quiet when near him. However, a very ironic aspect of this experience was that even though my dad would be abusive to mom, he would then constantly tell me to "not take shit from anyone." Over time, it became very obvious to me that his type of fatherly instruction was the initiator in creating my own belief system to hide my vulnerable side. This built the subconscious of "soft was for the weak" and "I'm TOO MUCH" which stifled my ability to speak softly from the heart.

In addition to the effects of a self-guarded dad, two separate difficult encounters happened around the ages of 4 to 5 years old. I was inappropriately put into compromised, intimate situations by two different men who were dad's "friends" at that time. How much do I remember of those moments? I can tell you exactly what happened, details of the external environment and also give you their first names. This added to the need for me to throw up my protection and self-guard.

Other significant factors that I can tie to my disposition, came with the fact that I grew up in a family that was largely male; a big brother, mostly boy cousins...you get my drift. My grandfather would say to me, "Now Sissy, you know girls aren't worth feeding." When my Pap became seriously ill, I mustered up the courage to ask him about this, and he told me that he was only joking.

Another occurrence supporting my insecurities happened at the age of 12. I was incredibly surprised to meet another young girl at church camp who had the same uncommon first name as me at the time. The initial excitement really hit until it was followed by her expressive reaction with a cringed face saying, "Your name is Brianne? Well, you can be the "Fat Bri" and I can be the "Skinny Bri." What could've been a loving response, turned into another reason to keep myself protected.

If you have been taking tally with what created my list of thoughts, feelings, and questions, you might be wondering what do I correlate to "feeling misunderstood, or I don't belong here?" Fasten your seatbelt, this part is interesting! I have the ability to connect and talk to the Souls and Presence on the Other Side. I'm a firm believer that we all possess this great gift from the instance our Source/God/Allah (or whatever great name you've chosen) gave life to our Soul. The Soul then continues inquisitively through its learnings within its physical body while still having support energetically with our Universal Team on the Other Side. I get asked quite a bit, "Do I need to learn how to concentrate on my Soul's connection with our Universal Team?" The answer is "no." I believe our Soul is always effortlessly in touch with the Other Side for guidance. So, if you are someone who focuses on your tangible senses during this journey then it just may be comforting to know that you're still connected on a greater level and have the support of our Universal Team. Ok, let me back up a second and define who our Universal Team is exactly. This just happens to be my way of having fewer words to describe our Source/God/Allah/whatever beautiful name you choose, Angels, Guides, Loved Ones, etc.

Many years were spent trying to figure out if I was crazy (talking to the Other Side) as well as if it was even worth being understood or receiving love. Then, the miraculous year of 2005 arrived and sparked a dissatisfied feeling within me. I felt a very strong, undeniable pull to leave everyone and everything that I knew in order to experience my own existence without influences. The funny question that constantly ran through my head during this "quarter life crisis" was, "Do I like Chinese food because I like it, or do I like it because my friends like it?" Later on, it became obvious to me that 2005 was when I began my proactive soul searching…my review, learning, adjusting and moving forward.

"NOW, WHAT DO YOU WANT TO DO WITH THIS?"

While continuing to review my journey, it became more apparent that the rare people I chose to be close friends to all possessed similar struggles when it came to matters of being vulnerable with trust and love. One of the most valuable concepts that I embraced was the understanding that all people, especially those who hurt me, had also experienced the same hurt if not worse in their own encounters. The concept of 'what people experience becomes their reality' truly brought on a much more caring and understanding position for me. Comprehending forgiveness occurred when watching others who were also going through their own challenges and then taking the time to view how I also presented myself outwardly.

For example, when I was put into the situation with two of my dad's friends, I heard one of my Guide's voices on the Other Side tell me how to get out of what was happening each time. Also, at the age of six, during a car accident where I almost went through the windshield, I heard a lady's voice from the Other Side tell me, "Ok Baby, hold on you're going to hit three times." She counted down each time and then stayed with me until my mom was by my side at the hospital. My last needed confirmation happened at the age of 18. I was diagnosed with Idiopathic Thrombocytopenic purpura (ITP). (I was given about a month to live if my autoimmune reaction couldn't be restricted on how it was destroying my platelets.) During that time, I lost a real sense of who I was and where my value came from.

I went from being very athletic and independent to having no strength, not being allowed to drive my own car, and hardly ever being alone just in case I started to bleed. A sense of pressure consumed me in wanting to hide my fears from my parents and brother. In my head, I saw this as displaying my strength to counter the devastation that I saw on their faces. The greatest peace I had during this time was having the Universal Team to talk to about my own fear and sadness. It was comforting to have them asking me, "Now, what do you want to do with this?" This magic question brought me back to a sense of feeling grounded and a deeper connection to my Soul's own power of choice.

Overall, the most difficult healing occurred while trying to grasp an understanding of "What is trust and love…is either real?" I definitely need to take you to the liberating part of that miraculous year. An important event that initiated my healing is one that most people have a tough time wrapping their heads around. However, it was one that gave me the first sense of peace that I was longing for. At the time, I had taken a temporary job as a Laboratory Scientist. During that assignment, I started to open up, make great connections and was having fun just living life. Since I had chosen to release my restricted self-preservation and overthinking, I jumped at the idea of supporting a co-worker who wanted to go see Mrs. A. She was a very caring, Gypsy, Grandma-like person who read Tarot cards as well as other things. Truthfully, I didn't have any intentions of having anything done for me. However, as things had finished with my co-worker, I felt the same pull and nudging that I felt while leaving my hometown. Even though a part of me felt so unsure about having cards done, I couldn't deny the attention-grabbing pull that I was feeling. So, I chose to follow my gut instinct. Every card drawn for me by Mrs. A. was on point to what I had experienced, was challenged in, and gave me great perspective as to what I might consider in the future. The greatest part came at the end of the session. Mrs. A. had asked me to think of a question in my head that I really wanted to have answered. "What does peace feel like?" rang loudly within my head. I was completely shocked when she surprisingly looked at me and said, "Child, you don't know what peace feels like?" After that moment, I decided to work with Mrs. A on discovering and healing the root cause of what I was longing for in my heart. She then worked up an aura chart which clearly showed the energetic connection I had with each of my parents and brother, the cause of my disconnect, the lack of feeling peace, and the questions that I had all my life regarding love and trust. It also gave me a much better understanding as to why my Soul stayed so focused and connected to the Other Side. With all of the details that were given to me, I could easily relate to the actual people, places and intuitive feelings that I had while growing up.

The deep situation that had unleashed a huge hurdle happened during my dad's alcoholic, unfaithful years. There was a waitress at the local bar who desperately wanted my dad and had gone to great lengths to try and break up my parents' marriage. She had actually gone to someone who considered themself a witch. Since my dad drank a lot then, it was easy for this waitress to get him to drink what the witch had made for her. Once he drank the mixture, the negative energies against my parents' ability to accept and receive love was then unleashed in the very moment that they had become intimate. The most interesting blessing that occurred which the waitress did not take into consideration was that I would be conceived by my mom in that exact moment and that my parents would fight hard to stay together for many more years to come. There were so many more details about my time with Mrs. A., and I trusted her to help me change this blockage within my life as well as helping to bring peace back to both my parents' lives if they allowed.

Now let's get to the man who I said "I do" to. Joe and I had officially met during 2005. At that point, I was 26 years old. When I left my hometown, I had no intention of committing to anyone but ME. During that time, I truly met my "mirror" in temperament. He and I both were driven, dominant, independent and stubborn. The attributes that he also possessed, of which I was drawn to, were his spontaneity, no regrets, unapologetic nature, and being an incredible 'man's man.' These were all attractive yet equally challenging traits when mixed with our commonalities. As time went on, we chose to commit as a couple. I began to learn more about what it was like to be loyal to a military man who was deployed multiple times and traveled globally within his civilian job. It was easy for me to come out of my more relaxed, easy-going mode and slip back into being the very precise, serious, supportive, grounding wire that I had previously been. For most of our relationship he was gone as much as he was home which suited our independent natures and more than likely kept my heart at a safe level from wanting to feel vulnerable and open. It's funny looking back at how it took six years of "playing house" before both of us even agreed that we could handle being married. Little did I realize then that there were still some deep, honest and vulnerable feelings that I had shoved down due to my self-protection which would boil up later on.

Thirteen years of being together we had our little boy. My husband took a new civilian job so he didn't miss any more amazing moments of our Miracle Muse's milestones as well as to be more of a constant support system to me. This was such a new territory for both of us especially since I never allowed myself to trust and depend on him for anything with him coming and going. Once we moved for his job, I had decided that I wanted to hang up my lab coat to become a stay-at-home mom for a while. Making the change from a Laboratory Scientist to full-time mommy highlighted some intense, self-preserving issues. One of the best questions to show up for me was, "Why did I keep Joe at arm's length even when he just made some tough decisions to change jobs, and didn't even hesitate to be the breadwinner to care for us?" It's as if I never realized all that he had sacrificed to be at home now with his family. I was able to whole-heartedly acknowledge and express how I felt during his scary deployments and civilian travels overseas without knowing if I ever would have him back home safely. I admitted to him and apologized that I also had kept him at arm's length because of all my past experiences with the men in my life. I began to realize that holding onto my past as today's reality was out of fear and it was blocking the blessings that had been waiting for me to embrace. I'm so grateful that we had this opportunity to learn how to open up our hearts, talk through our struggles and begin to trust past our self-protection fears.

One of the most phenomenal healings of the heart happened after years of not being able to conceive a baby. I endured an intense infertility process and pregnancy. Getting to see a positive pregnancy test was so shocking; like a dream that I was waiting to wake up from. My husband and I felt like we were being blessed with the most priceless gifts ever to be imagined - twins! Every second of this miraculous pregnancy, we held our breaths trying to be careful that only great things would come for them. However, at nine weeks of pregnancy, our saddest day happened. The doctor couldn't find the precious heartbeat of one of the twins and yet the other twin shined as bright as the Northern Star. After we walked out of the doctor's office, we just stared at each other without the ability to find words. I remember how my husband and I just sat in our truck stunned, numb, and then shifting into the most overwhelming cry. It was so confusing for our hearts to simultaneously shatter yet be so incredibly grateful at the same time. After that day, I stayed in the place of gratitude and thankfulness for the amazing little Soul who was continuing to choose me as his mommy. "WOW! So this is what love feels like," was the thought that kept running through my head as I touched my growing belly. Then another heart-felt challenge occurred at 24 weeks of the pregnancy when I received a crushing phone call from my aunt. She told me that my dad had passed away that morning; it was November 20th. It was as if the shock and grief of losing the other baby never left and then became heightened by what I had just heard. The only thoughts my poor body could process was, "F*ck…wait…?!?!"

LETTING GO OF CONTROL

In 2020, I anxiously began to open up to trust on a larger scale. An interesting thing is when the Universe is helping us blaze our trails, the majority of the time we are more focused on what's happening in any given moment than the greatness that's actually being unleashed as a result. For instance, the previous summer I took my son to the local park to play and there was another mother with her two little ones. There was such a sense of pull to her without any obvious reasons at the time. We came outside of our reserved natures and said "Hi" to one another. This became a pivotal moment that encouraged connecting, interacting and trusting others that I probably wouldn't have had the courage to do in the past. Her passion in establishing a women's group to obtain connections, support and guidance was the means for me to find my own confidence and "voice" within the masses. Also, it opened lanes for business mentors to come into my life as well as sparked the courage needed to vulnerably write about my experiences and put it out into the world. Even more importantly, I met and became friends with some of the most incredible and inspiring women I have ever met.

Lastly, I would love to share an extremely priceless event. This brought a feeling of coming full circle in life. Even though I know there's so much more to come, it's given me the opportunity to take what I've learned thus far and express it all within an intense yet interesting adventure.

The past three years, I began having anxiety attacks. Being that I had such a worrying, perfectionist and controlling nature, of course I'd have anxiety attacks. As time went on these episodes became more frequent with instances of my face drawing to the right side and then not being able to speak for several minutes after the episodes finished. After some routine blood work and an EEG to check my brainwaves, the last test was the key that brought the answers to light.

On Easter Sunday, I was scheduled to have an MRI done of my head. Since the other tests appeared promising for anxiety, my husband and I decided that he could just stay home with our son while I quickly went for the MRI. I was instructed to go to the Emergency Room entrance for registration since it was on a Sunday. Once there, the main ER desk attendant then told me that I actually needed to drive my car to the back of the hospital and go into a different entrance to be registered. This redirection initiated a difficult challenge of me letting go of control and trusting in the "strangers" to guide me in a facility that I had no familiarity with. The medical staff working at this location then informed me that I actually needed to go to the Radiology Department for outpatient MRI testing. At this point, I was stressed that I was going to be arriving late for my test. Thankfully, the MRI Tech graciously escorted me through another labyrinth of hallways to reach my destination. During my MRI, my dad showed up. Keep in mind he passed away to the Other Side a little over three years prior to this day. He held my hand and said, "Sissy, they're going to see some interesting things. Don't worry. You'll be alright. I'm by your side." When testing finished, I was guided back upstairs to the main Radiology Department and was asked to wait there to make sure they had everything that was needed for my test. After a 45 minute wait, the Radiologist spoke with me about the results. He said that I had a large, three centimeter tumor with tremendous swelling putting pressure on my brainstem. Everything went from a long, drawn out process to a whirlwind state.

I was escorted back to the Emergency Room. During this timeframe, I texted my family about the results I was given. Due to the size of my tumor and severe swelling, I was taken by ambulance to another big hospital. After making sure Gio was in the very best hands of my best friend, my husband joined my side. Even with the nonstop monitoring and processes going on with my care, the only parts that stuck out for me were the connections I made with my caregivers. I was even blessed to meet another "Brianne." She was my night shift nurse who was a beautiful mirror to me. Even with the COVID pandemic guidelines currently in place, it was amazing that my big brother, Will, was able to be by my side holding my hand through this health scare. Also, this moment gave back a sense of closeness with both sides of my family after feeling distanced for many years. Overall, Neurosurgery was a success and my Meningioma Tumor came back benign.

I've fallen in love with the most trying of years and events. They were all the exact seasons that my Soul was longing for in order to grasp such paramount understandings and healings. THANK GOODNESS!! Having a helpful way of viewing your own story can possibly help take some pain and frustration away while continuing to discover what you've needed to in order to see your life-changing truths.

As you go through all of your challenges and amazing "EUREKA!" moments, please hold onto this thought: We can't simply just check off the lessons learned within our great journey without understanding their inspirational value. Their purpose is to bring a deeper understanding of compassion and love for yourself as well as others.

I lift up my favorite drink to you, (CHEERS!!) let's take an incredible moment to celebrate YOU...for whole-heartedly stepping forward in being your own courageous powerhouse who is continuing to become more awake to what your Soul is here for!! Just know you're already on-point and doing amazing even if you feel otherwise! Your presence is priceless!! So, take some deep breaths and time-outs as you need, give yourself a high-five for continuing to be here on your journey and look forward to the blessings that are still waiting for you to embrace!! May every second from this moment on inspire you to fall deeper in love with yourself and all that your Soul is successfully learning!! You're on point, Darling!! Much love and many blessings.

SUPERHUGE HUGS

ACKNOWLEDGEMENTS

Thank you so much to my family and friends. Because of you, I have been blessed with the very best support and teachers in this life experience. I love you all! Also, much gratitude goes to all the other key players and catalysts that helped me to learn and grow into the person I continue to become.

ABOUT AUTHOR

Brianne "Bri" DiDino is the Founder of Beyond Grounded. She is a Certified Intuitive Life Coach with a passion and mission in being people's "spiritual cheerleader." She loves helping others to navigate and find understanding through their life experiences all while learning how to connect with the supportive Universal Team on the Other Side. She holds an Associate's degree in Applied Science with ASCP Board Certification for Medical Laboratory Technician as well as holds a Bachelor's degree in Applied Science for Biotechnology with ASCP Board Certification concentration in Microbiology. Also, she has completed her coach training at Robbins-Madanes Training under her teachers Tony Robbins, Cloe Madanes, Mark Peysha, and Magali Peysha.

ABOUT MY BUSINESS

The foundation for my business, Beyond Grounded, comes from all of my many life experiences thus far as well as being connected to our Universal Team on the Other Side since childhood. Whether I deemed my experiences as a negative challenge or a positive inspiration, one perspective encompasses it all for me…they are all blessings. Each moment has prepared, educated and inspired me to awaken to who I genuinely am and to do my life's purpose in helping and encouraging other individuals to uncover their true gifts and connections.

Website
https://www.beyondgrounded.com

Facebook Personal Page
www.facebook.com/beyondgrounded

Instagram
https://www.instagram.com/beyondgrounded/

THANK YOU!

If you are looking to reclaim confidence, get a clearer understanding and healing of past and current experiences, find a feeling of balance and joy when aligning yourself to your True Purpose, and/or longing to gain knowledge of the supportive Universal Team on the Other Side then I encourage you explore some options. On my website www.beyondgrounded.com, you can find links to schedule a FREE consult with me or to hear inspiring podcasts with remarkable Guests. Also, you can contact me at estella@beyondgrounded.com as well as find me on Facebook and Instagram.

Rachel Seltzner

ESCAPING THE PROM KING

It came out of the blue, while driving down Highway 16, returning to my then current residence after looking at a prospective new house. Two of my three children were in the back seat, and it happen in probably less than a blink of my eye, but it seemed like hours. A flash of a memory, a vision of sorts. This tiny snapshot of a moment in time brought a soul shaking earthquake of emotions I felt rattle my very core being. After the initial jolt, the resulting tsunami of realizations came as aftershocks, and they still continue to catch me off guard now, years later.

In this flash of realization, I came to understand the depth of my pain I had been pushing down below the surface to get through my days, my moments and try to put on a happy face to the world and for my children. With that flash, I saw and relived a moment of my (then) husband, the man who was supposed to love, honor, protect and respect me, force himself upon me. In the real moment of it happening, I didn't know it. I didn't understand it, and I certainly didn't put up a fight or even say no. Rage surged through me as I saw myself in that moment, allowing it to happen. Suddenly I understood that throughout nearly 15 years of marriage, I had been essentially brainwashed, slowly and stealthily. It felt so cold and calculated; but I was mad at myself, more than at him, for not seeing it more clearly sooner. All within this same heartbeat, I understood that I had been hiding myself, dissociating from my body and my thoughts, allowing any physical sensations I would have experienced at the time to just escape into the cosmos. It was easier than feeling the pain at the time, and it was way easier than the emotional repercussions I would have received in torment from him had I tried to resist him physically. A coping mechanism, I realized why I had done it, and granted myself a tiny bit of grace all in the same moment; I may not have lived through it otherwise.

My sweet little daughter's voice from the back seat snapped me back from what seemed a galaxy away in my mind, right back to the present moment. She asked, "So, Mom, when do you get your new husband?" We had just broken the news of the divorce a week or so prior, and here my daughter thought we'd just swing by the store and pick up a new dude for mommy like we'd bring home a goldfish from the county fair! I was about to launch into a whole long explanation of how that is not what divorce is about and it would probably be a long time before I even… "Because I really want my new sisters!" she interjected my thoughts. I may have managed to hide some of the shock in my response "Well, sweetie, there are no more babies coming out of this momma…" She quickly corrected me "No, Mom. Your new husband, he already has my TWO new sisters!" What? I could hardly imagine what she was thinking, especially as I was still trying to digest all of the wild, overwhelming, realizations I just had a moment ago.

We had already been living our separate lives within our shared (tiny!) home for several months now, and the house I had just looked at was where I could be moving to. I had created a makeshift bedroom for myself in the basement, hanging curtains from the floor joists, in an attempt to give myself a sense of privacy. The curtains did not offer protection though, and that was what I really needed at the time. One night, shortly after my big vision, I overheard him in the bathroom with our two youngest children. One of the children had accidentally stuck a toe in some grout work he had done recently and was still curing. The toe mark was still visible, but easily repairable. He had not told the kids about the grout, nor did they know it was drying and they shouldn't touch it. I didn't hear the exact words he used, but the tone of his voice is what I knew all too well. My daughter's cries and the look of terror in my son's eyes confirmed what my heart already knew. We had to get away, as soon as possible. I tried to kick him out of the house. I don't know where the sudden strength came from, but it was as if all the times he had used that voice with me, all the times he had forced himself upon me and every other wrong swelled up within me and told him that he was breaking our children's souls, and he had to leave NOW, and for good. After a threat of calling police, he finally left the house. In my gut, I knew he'd be back, and would probably return drunk.

I REALIZE NOW

Before we married, I realized he was an alcoholic. I recognized that when he drank, he not only couldn't stop until he passed out, but he also turned into a raging, oozing with multiple hemorrhoids, asshole. It was unmistakably worse than his usual bad attitude. After one particularly nasty incident that resulted in my sobbing in the shower for nearly an hour, I told him I wouldn't marry him if he was still drinking. He promptly up and quit beer and booze just like that. My naïve brain thought he must really deeply love me to be able to give that up so quickly, for me. What I didn't understand was that he was still alcoholic, without drinking, and that just giving up the drink didn't solve any of the problems. Within a few months of our marriage, he was back to the bottle, jumping straight from his previous 30 pack of beer a night to entire bottles of whiskey in one sitting.

A few weeks before getting married, I had moved to another state, 1500 miles away from my home and family. We planned to start our new married life there together, but the new job didn't want to wait for me. So I moved, flew home for a long weekend to get married, and then returned to my lonely apartment for what I called our reverse honeymoon. He didn't have a job in our new area yet, but did at home for 2 months, so stayed through that, then joined me. He quickly found a job in his profession, which was quite exciting as those type of jobs tend to be rare and tough to get into – that was part of the reason we decided the move was worth it, for both of us to find work we loved. We had agreed that to move that far, we were committed to staying for at least two years, so I suggested we buy a house. It took quite a bit of convincing but he finally agreed and we closed on our first home before having to renew the apartment lease and moved in.

Getting settled into the house felt like we had arrived in the world! We were in our early twenties, we both had great jobs we loved, in our fields, and we owned a nice home! As we were getting established and making names for ourselves, we were also making new friends and creating our new network. After a fun night out with friends, he lamented the fact he "couldn't" have a drink, you know, just to be social. The way he talked about it, I realize now, was to make me feel at fault somehow, as if I was the one controlling his choices. I very clearly stated to him at the time that if he wanted to have a drink (and I emphasized that as ONE drink) and he felt he could do that without feeling compelled to drink more and let the alcohol control him, that was his choice. I also reminded him how much he had hurt me previously when he was drunk, and I wasn't up for repeating any of that.

All too predictably, I suppose, the next social night out, he decided to have a drink. But he promised me he would only have one early, and he would drive us home, so I could be free to have fun and enjoy as desired. That was the night I drove him home and he passed out in the car on the way, after he spent a night pounding drinks, berating me in front of new friends, and generally making a complete ass of himself. I contemplated just leaving him in the car when I pulled in the driveway. We had taken my car, my brand new car. The first NEW car of my entire LIFE. I didn't want him to puke in the brand new car or anything else, so I decided I'd just drag him out of the car and leave him lying there in the carport, locking him out of the house. When I opened the car door, he fell out and it roused him enough that he was able to drag himself into the house. The thought crossed my mind about kicking him out of the house, but I wondered where he would go or how he could get anywhere in his current condition. I certainly didn't have another place to go either, so in the house he came, and I just made myself more upset about the situation. This vicious cycle of him drinking, attempting to "apologize" and promising it would never happen again kept going for years. Being the eternal optimist I am, every time he promised to be better, I believed him; or at least I wanted to believe him, knowing in my heart it probably wasn't true. After returning from a special work event over a long weekend, I returned home, expecting him to be at a work event of his own. Instead, I found many empty bottles of alcohol throughout the house, a huge mess on my desk including Jack Daniels bottles and dried liquor spills all over my computer. In the kitchen, I found more spills and stains, and a journal from my college years open on the counter, also with fresh whiskey stains all over it.

Finally finding him, passed out on the bathroom floor with another truly indescribable mess, I checked to make sure he was still alive. I was honestly shocked to find him still breathing. I had no idea how long he had been there or how much he had drank. Once he roused himself, he started berating me, calling me awful names and accusing me of horrific things. These early years of marriage, I found myself praying repeatedly for him to "just hit me." For some reason, in my head, that seemed to be a concrete, tangible line that would prove that the way he was treating me was unacceptable. I'm a very spiritual person, not particularly religious, and can't remember a time I had really prayed before that. I thought anyone would understand that's not okay, and I could divorce him and move on, if he would just hit me already, please for the love of God! Can you imagine hurting so badly that you're praying for someone to physically harm you because that pain would be easier to manage? He wouldn't just hit me, but the threat of physical harm was always there. Having been trained in law enforcement, he would "demonstrate" to me how easily he could disarm someone or incapacitate them if needed. One particular move involved a thumb pressed into the neck just so, and could take a person to the floor in a moment. A thumbs up sign in our marriage took on a very different meaning than what an outsider would have expected.

I spent so many years trying to love him more, thinking I could save him, or help him become better. So many years thinking that divorce would be giving up, and failure. When my little boy begged me to "divorce Daddy, so we can run away" I told him divorce was not an option and people who love each other work things out. I thought it was best for children to have both parents living together. Now, I realize how our toxic relationship was ruining my children – and it was my breaking point to finally give me the strength and courage to leave. Realizing I could not let my daughter grow up thinking she could allow someone to treat her this way; and I certainly wasn't going to allow my sons to continue this in their potential future relationships made me understand that breaking this awful cycle and divorcing him would not be me failing, it would be me winning; for myself, for my children, and even for him. There was only so much love I could offer him; he would have to heal himself on his own.

As a young gal, I was one of those ultra-independent, headstrong types. I did my own thing, had my own toolbox, went wilderness camping – alone – and generally had no time for others telling me what to do. I wasn't really into finding a relationship, and released my college boyfriend because I felt too constrained. He was a great guy, not controlling at all, no red flags; I just didn't want to feel restricted by a commitment. Considering relationships that became abusive, I didn't understand how people would allow themselves to get into that situation. "Just get rid of his dumb ass, don't put up with that shit!" I would say. But I now understand the nuances of how an abusive relationship works. It doesn't just start that way. He "love bombed" me, going over the top to show me what an incredible guy he was. He was well liked at work and in our social group; we had many mutual friends in college, though we didn't meet until after graduating. As soon as he thought I was hooked, he started the tiny remarks here and there. I often chalked it up to him being drunk, not recognizing it happened more frequently than that. Then he started with the bigger remarks and the physical threats. He would always apologize and swear to do better for the future. And he would do better, for a short time. Just enough to hook me back in, thinking he had really, finally changed this time. And then he'd really surprise me with a doozy. When I suspected him of cheating, due to evidence on our shared home computer, he jumped to a jealous rage, though I never gave him any reason to be jealous or suspicious of me. If I questioned him about something I was upset about, he would tell me it never happened, or relate a completely different version of reality to me. It was so extreme, I started to question my own sanity at times. Then guess what? He started calling me crazy! Now, I recognize this as gaslighting; he was purposefully trying to make me think I was losing my mind.

I AM DONE

Day by day, month by month, year by year, he was insidiously tearing away at me; trying to control me, trying to make me conform to his idea of what I should be. When I finally started waking up to his tricks, I took back my power. I started repeating the things he said to me and proclaimed my nonacceptance of it. He still tried to deny my reality. I started recording our conversations and playing it back to him. "Why yes, you DID call me a fu*k!ng whore" for having a boyfriend in college before I met you. PS: I never even slept with him. (Rewind the recording) "There it is – in your voice! Are you telling me that's NOT what you said? Was there someone else in the room disguising their voice as yours? You DID say it, you meant it, along with all the other nasty things you've said and done to me over the past 15 years, and I AM DONE."

To help with my healing, and to process all that I've been through, I started writing. Or better put, I started writing even more. Flashbacks of the pain and trauma –

emotional and physical started pouring out. I confronted him about raping me. He of course took the victim role for himself and asked me how he should now deal with the idea that he's a rapist. I apologized. I APOLOGIZED! WHAT?!?! Clearly, I had more healing to do. I only mention this to give you an understanding of how incredibly he affected my thought process, and how our brains attempt to protect us while in survival mode. Shortly after that encounter, I laughed out loud at myself, hysterically. It turned into cry laughing, but they were healing tears. One day while working through divorce proceedings, I called my mom in frustration. I don't even remember what the particular issue was at the time, but my mom just replied "well that PROM KING is just gonna have to get it through his head that…" and I had a lightbulb moment! I would use all my pain to help others dealing with situations like this in a book, and it would be called Married to the Prom King! About 7 years into our marriage, I discovered he had been the prom king in high school. I was flabbergasted! Not because of him being prom king; but that I had somehow found myself married to a prom king of all people! I was not the prom going type in high school. I only went to prom my senior year at my friend's insistence that I would make it way more fun. In my typical style, I showed up to prom in a tie-dyed polyester dress with blue sparkly jelly shoes! And there I was, so many years later, married to a prom king? It seemed surreal and hilarious.

Trying to decide how to categorize Married to The Prom King, I started calling it my autobiographical self-help comedy horror novel. The title seemed too perfect. In public, he was all the things most people expect from a

Prom King; he was the popular, athletic, likable guy that everyone wanted to hang around with. But to me, he embodied all the awful stereotypical things I thought of prom kings at the time – conceited, entitled, rude, narcissistic and unkind. As always with me, my story of marrying and eventually escaping the Prom King is a hilarity filled adventure of self-discovery and growth. I have so much more to get down on the page, but I took a slight break while creating the stories that will be in Prom's Over, Post Prom Party, and the yet-to-be-titled culmination where I have found my true king. He embodies all the fairy tale like qualities you'd expect in a prom king; a calm leader, introspective and self-reflective, honorable, respectful and caring. Oh, and incredibly handsome to boot! And, interestingly enough (though not a prom king quality), he's got 2 daughters.

Along with writing and sharing my story, a big part of my healing process was what I call #ReviveCrazyRach! One of the first nights out to have fun with some friends after splitting from the prom king sparked the name. I related to a long time friend how miserable I had been for so long and I didn't feel like myself anymore. She said "but you're CrazyRach!" recalling how I was referred to in our college days, and how everyone looked to me for fun times. She and I immediately hatched my plan to bring joy back into my life by getting back to doing all the fun things I had enjoyed before marriage. The concert we were on our way to wound up being the first documented #ReviveCrazyRach event. Realizing the power this had in my own life, I created a program through my work, to help others bring joy back into their lives as well. Having devoted so much of my life to helping others with their physical health, I was saddened when I asked so many of them what their newfound health would bring them in life, and how they too had been so disconnected from joy in their lives. Now, my Wildly Grounded program not only helps others find their best physical health, but it helps them enjoy life to the fullest too! The smiles, laughter and profound positive changes I've seen come about from others getting Wildly Grounded is fulfilling in so many ways, and has helped to fuel my own transformation as well.

It would have been so easy to play the victim through all of this, and I was a victim. The process to change and transform has not been easy, but the CHOICE to change and take my power back was simple. All it really took was the spark of inspiration and me changing my mindset. I saw divorce as failure. But a true failure would have been letting him completely ruin me if I had stayed. A failure would have been allowing my children to continue to grow up in that toxic environment and think that's what is normal. A failure would have been staying. I chose divorce as a win. A win for myself, a win for my children, a win for my family for generations to come. It's never perfect, but the cycle has stopped. I choose a better future, and so can you; whether it is an abusive relationship or a toxic work environment. Recognize what truly is a failure or a win. Choose to win, and create your plan to go get it!

ACKNOWLEDGEMENTS

To my family and friends who have supported me throughout life: I hope to be able to express my profound gratitude and love to you in our day-to-day lives, so that you always know how important you are to me! Each of you provided fuel to my transformational fire along the way. Special thanks to my yoga teacher friends and instructors who were with me in the thick of my healing process and will forever hold a special place in my heart. My sweet children are the brightest lights of my life and were sometimes my only spark in the darkest of moments, I could only dream to have the depth of expression to share your meaning with you. And to this incredible man who gave my fragile heart the softest place to land with gentle understanding, and provided space to heal and trust again... I would shed all of my tears a thousand times again if I had to, to find your love. Shout out to the musicians whose music and lyrics helped carry me through dark times, and whose performances helped #ReviveCrazyRach, especially: 311, Tropidelic, G. Love and Special Sauce and Ben Harper; you are the soundtrack of my life. To everyone I have worked with: I thank you so much for your trust and confidence in me to help you improve your health and bring more joy into your life. Know that I'm honored, and your story has helped me and others on their path as well. To anyone struggling in a toxic relationship, please find your spark to ignite your own transformation. Reach out to a trusted professional or a friend to get started if you need to; be safe! Get Wildly Grounded, deepen your roots, grow more joy! To quote my favorite band, 311, "Stay Positive and Love Your Life!"

ABOUT AUTHOR

Rachel Seltzner, ND, PhD, is a board certified Naturopath, certified Yoga Instructor and a self-proclaimed nature nut. She is on a mission to make the world a better place by helping others feel their best! Integrating holistic health and lifestyle therapies, nature therapy and yoga, Dr. Rachel helps others create physical health and find more joy in their lives.

ABOUT MY BUSINESS

Dr. Rachel coined the term Wildly Grounded to convey her passion for nature and a healthy lifestyle. Being Wildly Grounded means being rooted in nature and healthy lifestyle practices so that you can branch out and blossom into YOUR most beautiful expression of yourself!

Website
www.WildlyGrounded.com

Facebook Personal Page
WildlyGrounded

Instagram
NaturallyRachND and CrazyRachey79

THANK YOU!

Thank You so much for reading the Don't Be Invisible, Be Fabulous book, and my story! Please reach out to me on Facebook, Instagram or rachel@wildlygrounded.com for a special free consult to discover how you can get Wildly Grounded with me!

Lisa Condon

LIVING OUT LOUD

I left hospice at about 11:30 pm. My husband had left earlier to drive the 3 hours home to take care of our cat, as we had just relocated a few weeks prior. I was going to the hotel to get some rest. Only a half hour after falling asleep did I get the call, that my Dad had passed away. I knew it was coming, as the day prior he saw his Mom out his window, of which she had passed away in 2003. Yet, you aren't ever ready for the passing of a parent. Moreover, you really aren't ready for the passing of your second parent – especially when you are in your 30's.

Right after my 33rd birthday, I received a call that my Mom was heading to the emergency room because her heart rate was very high. As I was living more than 500 miles away, there was nothing I could do but wait to hear what the Dr's said. The next call was a few hours late to tell me they were admitting her for observation. Given my Mom's stubborn spirit, this was a good thing in my book. That evening I chatted with her, and she was in fantastic spirits. The Dr's were getting her heart rate stabilized and she was to be released the following day. The next morning, I called her hospital room, and no one answered.

I assumed she was going in for tests, so I headed to my leadership meeting knowing I would call her afterward. When I did, she answered and the voice on the other end of the phone was frightened. It was that moment that my Mom told me they had done a Pet Scan and they were putting together a plan to treat her for cancer, small cell lung cancer to be exact. A complete shock to me, I told her I was getting on the next plane home. And I did. I will skip the part where my ex-husband said, "well, what do you want me to do about it" when I called to let him know my Mom was sick. Somehow, I got myself home, got on a plane, had my best friend pick me up and drive to the hospital. It took longer than expected, as in haste, a few wrong turns were made out of the airport; but I got there. For the next ten days, we got her through initial treatments and determined the plan. I got her home, and between my brother, her best friend, and myself – everything was in place. It came time for me to head home, after two and a half weeks. When she and her best friend dropped me at the airport, I didn't know it would be the last time I saw her. From symptom to death, only five weeks went by.

Within a six-year span, I had lost both of my parents, of whom I was close with. Both within a short period of time, in fact just 5 weeks from symptom to death, each. To say that this impacted my life is an understatement.

I FORGOT WHAT I PROMISED

The lessons I learned, though, as I reflect, and age are incredibly important and valuable for my own life journey.

First, there is something freeing about the day you become an orphan. Now, don't get me wrong, I miss my parents every day. Yet, it's amazing how you hold onto things like not wanting to disappoint well into adulthood. I was lucky that my parents were supportive and continually encouraged me to excel and be independent. I was unlucky that I came from an incredibly competitive family, particularly in sports. So, I found myself growing up always wanting to be the best in everything I did and feeling inadequate when I didn't win. In fact, I remember an election in elementary school where I was running for president of my third-grade class. I didn't win and my good friend, Missie, did. I was so upset that I threw a chair in the classroom. I am still embarrassed by that reaction to this day, but I was so disappointed in myself that I had no other way to express my emotion.

These types of outward reactions lessened over the years; but inside I still beat myself up for anything less than perfection. I found that my head and my heart disassociated from one another, leaving me to focus on school and ultimately work, where I could easily show growth by good grades or climbing the corporate ladder. Looking back, my parents would have been proud of me for whatever I did; this was the pressure I put on myself to be the best version of me…for them.

So, after my Mom transitioned, I changed. I vowed to live life to the fullest, to find happiness, to seek adventure and to live my true authentic self. And, I did. I met my now husband a year later, I left a job that was bringing me no joy and I blossomed. But, as time goes on, I forgot what I promised myself. I was still living at a higher vibrancy than I once did, with the man who was and is the keeper of my heart; yet I was not living everything about my life to the fullest. I was not "Living Out Loud."

When Nate and I first started dating, I told him that I wanted to live near my Dad before anything ever happened. Nate, being the ultimate adventurer, was all in. So, for two years we looked at property in my old hometown of Lancaster, Pennsylvania and at the beach in Delaware where my Dad frequented. I remember very clearly saying that if I was leaving Vermont, it would be for the ocean. So, we did. What an adventure! We literally knew no one, packed our home and moved to Delaware in 2013. We were so happy and excited to make new memories with my Dad, and to be closer to my best friend. Three hours was better than ten. A little over a week after we moved, my Dad called to let me know he was having some pain and he was planning to see a Dr. My Dad had not been to a Dr. in over 30 years to get looked at, so I knew the pain was serious. The next few weeks went something like this: lots of Dr appointments that his girlfriend took him to and from, placement in the hospital for testing, diagnosis of mesothelioma and lung surgery. After recovery, he said he wanted to recover at the home of his girlfriend, against my and my brother's better judgement. But he did. We got him home and settled. I then went back to my home in Delaware for a night of reprieve, as I had been the primary healthcare advocate. In the middle of the night, I got a call. My Dad had fallen, and they couldn't get in touch with my brother who lived nearby. I did. I asked him to go and check out Dad and I would be there in the morning. In the morning, after conversations, I made the decision to call an ambulance, as it sounded like my Dad was hurt. Sure enough, he had broken ribs. I got to the hospital, and all my Dad wanted to do was go home. He had just gotten out. So, we got him home, I stayed until we found a company that could do in-home care. We also contacted hospice, as my Dad chose to not do any life-prolonging procedures. The night before Thanksgiving, we had the first in-home provider stay. I stayed in a hotel with Nate and his Mom, so we could have Thanksgiving together the next day. It would have been the first Thanksgiving with my Dad since I was 12. I was very excited. Thanksgiving morning, I drove to his house to relieve the aid, and within minutes my Dad was groaning in agony. I called hospice and the nurse came within the hour. Watching anyone in that much pain is excruciating when it's someone you love it's devastating. She could not get his pain under control, so she called the ambulance to take him to the hospice facility. It's where I spent my time the next week and a half until he passed away. Once again, I felt the pull to "Live Out Loud."

I REMINDED MYSELF

I was a mess. I was now an adult with no parents. I had not realized how much influence they had on my life, as I constantly checked in for their opinions, reactions, and guidance. Now, it was all me. Was I making the right decisions? Had I not left my Mom alone and monitored her progress, would she have been alive longer? Why did I think work was more important than relationships? How could I be thinking about the fact that now we lived in

Delaware knowing no one? I felt the need to be the best daughter, still. I didn't want to disappoint my parents who were gone by making wrong decisions. It was a lot of pressure on myself.

Then, one day, it all lifted.

I reminded myself of who I was. My Father's daughter and my Mother's pride. I was exactly who I was meant to be. My parents raised me to be independent, announcing at the ripe old age of five that my future self would leave the small town of Lancaster, PA to live in the city. Even then I knew I was meant for a bigger world. And so, at age 17, I left for college and never looked back. Only a short stint in 2001, after I watched the towers fall from my office window, did I retreat home. I leaned on my parents differently those two weeks - my Mom to take care of me, my Dad to understand me. I learned a lot about what it meant to be family those few weeks. I learned a lot about me. After their deaths, I learned even more. These lessons are what I want to share with you.

> **You will always care what your parents think.** As much as none of want to admit it, as independent as you may be…you care. There are moments where you will have choices to make and how your parents will view it will play into the decision you make. They are often the voice in your head and the angel on your shoulder. Embrace it, for these are the individuals who you learned the basics from. Not only what to do, but also what not to do.

After your parents leave this earth, the concerns you carry around change. You begin to realize how proud they would be of the things you have accomplished. Small things, big things. For me, this usually happens when I find myself completely content in the moment I am in. I look out at the ocean and wish my Dad were with me to enjoy it. I plan an adventure and all I want is to share it with my Mom. The life you are given in this go around is what you make of it. If you spend your time worrying, you will miss life happening all around you.

Your story does matter. No matter how beautiful or how dark it has been, it is yours to share as you choose. This was something I wish I understood while my parents were still alive. I censored myself a lot because I didn't want to hurt them. As a bad-ass survivor of childhood sexual abuse, I didn't start sharing pieces of my story until after my Mom passed in 2007. I didn't talk about the events in any detail until after my Dad passed in 2013. I was protecting them from my story, when in fact it would have brought us closer as a family.

Family is the one you create. Not every person has a stellar relationship with one or both of their parents. In fact, not very person has a stellar relationship with most or all their family. What I believe is that family is not about blood. It is about the people you bring into your life. The ones you show all your scars and bruises to. The ones you share your most joyous moments with. The ones that will hold your hand and cry in silence. Family is not by blood but by choice. I am so grateful that I found the staple of my chosen family when I was twelve. For 35 years, she has been through it all with me and I with her. And as our lives have grown with marriage and children, the family expands.

Living in your authenticity is powerful. I went through many internal battles of being who I am vs. being a version of myself. The reality is that when you are truly you, the right people are in your life for the right reasons. I trust the universe will always give me what I need.

So, while I was an independent, free spirit at heart; I conformed myself to the needs of what I thought others had of me. Who I thought my parents expected me to be. Yet, when all is said and done, what people really needed and truly wanted was me. Talk about vulnerable. They still need that, and I now love giving that vulnerability to those in my life. It has brought me closer to those I love and to those I choose to share my time, energy, and space. As I live authentically and unapologetically, I am a model for my Godchildren, for other people who silence themselves in the name of perfection, who forget that the best gift you can give anyone is you. I embrace the pain of loss and the joy of change. I am, finally, "Living Out Loud."

ACKNOWLEDGEMENTS

To Nate who inspires me every day to be the best version of myself

ABOUT AUTHOR

Lisa is a certified Six Sigma Black Belt, SCRUM Master, Certified Scrum Product Owner, and PMP. By combining her love of creativity and her passion for process, she is the founder and creator of GRATITUDE, a proprietary program designed to spark change. She is the author of the soon-to-be released book, "Sparking Your Business, 9 Steps of Gratitude"

ABOUT MY BUSINESS

Lisa Condon Enterprises is a company that sparks inspiration, innovation, and collaboration through gratitude. Founder and motivational speaker, Lisa, uses a combination of theory and practices from the Project Management Institute, Six Sigma, SCRUM, EQi, and Appreciative Inquiry to build a sustainable growth strategy for you and your business.

Website
www.LisaCondon.com

Facebook Personal Page
https://www.facebook.com/lisacondonspark

Instagram
linktr.ee/lisacondonspark

THANK YOU OFFER!

Free 30 Minute Strategy Session

Giselle De Sousa

LIVE YOUR TRUTH...
YOU ARE MEANT FOR MORE

The Power Of Choosing You

I am the woman I am today because of my story I am about to share with you. I did not let myself give up even when it felt as if there was no way out. I had two reasons and they mean more to me than anything. Those reasons would be my two beautiful girls. When I look at them, I see beauty, strength, determination, love, and know in my heart they were the greatest blessings through a time in my life that for most would be hard to bear. My daughters would be the reason I survived. My past is not my future. How we take those moments that are made to break us is what matters. We must find the strength and have faith to know there is more for us. We are capable of so much more than we give ourselves credit for. I have realized in all of the moments, as hard as it was, I wouldn't have the two most amazing gifts that I am lucky enough to call my daughters today. They were the reason I was able to get through all of it and they gave me the strength. Looking at them I knew I had to be the woman who wanted more for them and myself. I couldn't just be in the situation I was in. I had to be the woman to take a stand, find her voice and leave. I didn't want my girls to think this is the way a man should treat a woman. The cycle could not continue. I came from a strong close family where family and marriage were everything. Divorce was not something I knew anything about. I knew in the end if I didn't leave, I might not be here today to share my story.

We can let situations either break us or help us to a higher purpose. We are not defined by what people tell us. We are defined by ourselves. I was destined for more. I knew there was a reason for everything I've been through. I now know I am meant to share this story with you the one reading this. My story might not pertain to you but more than likely you know someone that might need to hear this or are in a similar situation. I am a powerful confident strong woman surrounded with love. I am self-sufficient and know I can accomplish anything. This was not always the case. There was a time when I really didn't know what love was. I was young and in love or what I thought love was. I thought I had it all and looking back I was so blinded. I guess I should probably tell my story so you can understand. I was in my junior year of high school. I had a new car, many great friends, and life was everything it should be. I went to all the high school activities and loved life. I came from a household where family was everything. My parents always instilled in me a strong work ethic. They always gave us an abundance of love and the belief that anything was possible if you put your mind to it. My parents were a team and it didn't matter what it was they did it together. I grew up having everything I ever needed. I knew what love was firsthand. I saw it and received it from my parents and my brothers. My junior year summer is when one encounter would lead me to two of my greatest joys and some of my worst moments. I would doubt my values, morals, and the love of my family and myself and it would all start with that encounter. In my junior year summer, I would meet who I believed would be the man I was going to spend the rest of my life with. Growing up I always knew I wanted to be married and fanaticized about the day of my wedding and being a mom. When we are young, we see everything in life as being perfect. It's as if we take scenes out of a movie of what we think life and love should be. We believe it's so much that we turn it into a reality or so we think.

One thing I have learned is you can never change anyone. Why would you? If you are changing someone then are you in love with them or who you want them to be? I always thought if you loved enough and showed them how much you love them that they should want to change. I never understood in my younger years how you can love them till there is nothing left in you and yet it will not be enough. That is what we must pay attention to. I look back at that seventeen-year-old that would make that encounter and think I just believed in love. I'm sure as you read my story you will wonder why didn't she just leave? Why did she stay? Did she not see it? Love can be a crazy thing it can bring us to the highest of highs or lowest of lows. Those are always questions, that people ask when they haven't found themselves in an abusive situation. I see it now. I did not see it then. When you are in a situation whether it's emotional or physical abuse or both it normally isn't in an overnight occurrence. Many abusers slowly bring in the victim over time it's as if you lost all rhyme or reason. They make you believe that your thoughts are crazy. It's definitely narcissistic behavior at its best. It would all start with meeting a 17-year-old boy one night when cruising was a thing. I know I am dating myself here. We instantly would hit it off and started talking on the phone all the time. We lived in different cities and attended different high schools. Through the summer we would start dating and going back and forth to see each other as much as we could. I would start my senior year excited for the future. Senior year was the year full of celebration of senior events and the promises of what was ahead. I was excited about my new boyfriend and everything was exactly how it should be at school and in my life. Who knew what was ahead of us?

In a moment it would all change January of my senior year. My boyfriend at the time mentioned he wasn't feeling well and noticed petechiae on his legs and his Doctor rushed him in for tests. The next few days would be agony just waiting for tests to come back. He was too young to have anything really wrong with him, or was he? I will never forget the day the results came in. I was sitting in health class and my teacher Mrs. Wolfe was speaking about the topic of domestic violence, the stats on it, and what to look for. I remember specifically thinking and leaning over to tell my friend next to me that will never be me. I would never let someone treat me that way. I knew better or so I thought. I would be in that class when my pager would go off. Yes, I am aging myself again. No, we did not have cell phones back then. I knew it was him and his results were back. I would leave class for a moment to call him on the phone. I called him and he spoke of his results and his diagnosis and I instantly broke down crying. I headed back to my classroom confused with tears in my eyes. I will always be grateful to my teacher for her grace and calmness during a time that I was completely distraught and scared. She would ask me what was wrong. I would tell her my boyfriend had just been diagnosed with leukemia. Saying it out loud with my own words made it so real. That would be a pivotal moment that would change so much. He would start treatment immediately at UC Davis. He would be diagnosed with the worst form of Leukemia at the age of 17 years old. We sat there together in UC Davis as the Doctor told us his chances of survival were slim and him making it would be a miracle. I was in denial and was not going to accept that. I had a strong faith and believed he would somehow make it out. I always believed love conquers all.

I would spend the next six months going back and forth to the hospital and at the same time finishing my senior year. He would go through chemotherapy treatments with me by his side. I remember one day the Doctor coming in and telling us he will never have kids if he makes it because of the chemotherapy potency. I was devastated. I knew I wanted to be a mom, wife and have the family my parents gave us all growing up. I always kept faith despite the odds. The nurses would give me the nickname Green Eyes and would set up a bed in the nurses' quarters for me when I would stay. I was committed to being by his side through it all. He miraculously survived cancer that originally was his death sentence. His fight for survival would bring us that much closer as a couple. I would end up not attending senior activities outside of school. The thought that you can lose someone so easily shook me hard.

A LOT WOULD CHANGE

We would move in together and build a life after we graduated from high school. My parents weren't excited. My focus was on him and hoping that his cancer never would come back. Watching him survive cancer made me appreciate life that much more. I thought wow he survived something that could have killed him. He had to find this as a blessing and have a new lease on life. The complete opposite happened. He felt that people owed him for what he went through. I realized when someone goes through something like cancer, they either choose to make their lives better or worse. He chose the latter. I didn't realize it at the moment but there was something that started changing in him. I couldn't put my figure on it. I chalked it up to we are just young and newly living together. I had planned our whole future together.

Fast forward to nineteen years old and I discovered I am pregnant with my older daughter. Our miracle baby. What they said would never happen did. I was overjoyed. We again defeated the odds. Was I nervous because I was so young? Of course, but I knew I was always meant to be a mom. I wanted to have a child with him after all that we went through. I wanted to give him the gift of life. We were so excited about the new baby coming. I knew our baby would have an abundance of love. She would end up being one of my greatest joys and blessings in my life. She would be the voice that would save me in the end. I did not see any warning signs at first. I was so in love. He would get mad often. It's as if his anger was a light switch flipping on and off as quick as the flip of the switch. He didn't have the greatest family upbringing or friends. I felt as if I could give it all to him. I could show him true love and what a family was. I was so naïve in so many ways. I was a child at nineteen now going to raise a child of my own. My child and I were going to grow up together. I always felt so much older than my age. I remember my dad coming up to me at our family business when I was 18 years old. He said to me, "You need to manage the business. One day I won't be here. If you're not here at the business to manage it. It will go under." I told him, "but my older brother is here he can manage the business." He again repeated, "it has to be you or it will go under." He was teaching me how to manage businesses before I was 18 years old. Having a child at such a young age didn't even phase me it just seemed like the next step. If my dad believed I could manage and eventually own the businesses I knew anything was possible. I had so much going for me. A lot would change over time.

One particular night I still remember as if it was yesterday. There was something that set him off and he went into a rampage. I was pregnant with our oldest child at the time. He got in my face and seeing the anger in his eyes was terrifying. He would end up pushing me so hard in a fit of rage that I hit the couch with my back. I was so upset crying and crushed he would ever hurt me and let alone possibly hurt our child I was carrying. All I could think about was I don't want to lose our baby. I instantly went into being a mom and wanted to protect my child. He would threaten me and eventually, after pushing me against the couch he walked out the door. The moment he walked out I tried to lock the door behind him. He would try to force the door open with me behind it. All I could think was he might either hurt me or even kill me with the rage I saw in his eyes. I luckily was able to push with all of my strength to get the door locked that he was aggressively trying to push open. He was yelling from outside the door. He eventually came to the backyard and tried to get through the sliding glass door. He kept telling me to let him in or else. I was so scared of what he might do. I honestly was terrified for my life and my child's. I yelled at him, "you need to leave or I am calling the police." No one should ever have to say that to someone they are with. Ever! I did end up calling the police because I was so scared that something was wrong with our baby and feared for my life. He would eventually leave for the night. I would ride in the back of the police car to the hospital. On the way, the police officers were speaking and questioning me about what happened. They were trying to explain to me that this isn't right. This is not what love is and I need to leave. They told me, "he will do this again. You might not be as lucky next time." I didn't want to believe that. I thought what have I gotten into. I checked into the ER immediately and ran tests. They gave me a fake name for protection. They had mentioned abusers at times will come to find you. The nurses take notes and take pictures of the bruises on my body. I couldn't believe I was Jane Doe and my case was labeled as domestic violence. The nurses reiterated what the police officers said. The police officers came into my room and asked if I wanted to press charges. I was so confused, exhausted, sad, and in disbelief of what had happened. It was as if it was just a bad dream. I had so many emotions in that moment.

I told them, "I can't press charges. He's the father to my baby and I love him. This just was a mistake a misunderstanding." The nurses would come back and tell me my baby was unharmed. That was the most joy and the only joy I had that night was hearing those words. The police officers would end up driving me back home against everyone's advice. I would sit there in our place scared to sleep and not sure what to do next. He would end up coming home the next day and say how sorry he was. How it will never happen again. Please don't leave me. I love you. I was wrong. Abusers will always tell you they will change. That they were wrong and it will never happen again. They give you a lot of empty promises or make you believe in some way you are to blame. They are experts in manipulation. I kept everything quiet from my family and his. I didn't want my family to know. It would devastate my parents if they knew what I was going through. When you are in an abusive relationship you are so blinded to reality. I believed the words he said that day. I wanted it to be a one-time occurrence. I wanted my child to have a family, not a broken family. I grew up with my parents married forever. I didn't see that one night would be the red flag of many that I should have paid attention to. What if I leave and his cancer comes back or something happens to him? I couldn't have that on me. I held guilt. I had put so much pressure on myself. I always thought of him and his well-being.

I never once stopped and realized I was sacrificing myself. I would end up having my beautiful baby girl. The first time they looked at each other there was this love. I thought him being a father had to bring a change in him. We would end up getting married shortly after. He always longed for love. He grew up watching his mom go through abuse with his dad and he also was abused by his stepfather. I wanted to give him the life I grew up with. My parents always sensed something wasn't right. They were as supportive as they could be because they loved my child and me. There was a time before I had my daughter that my parents and him had got into a disagreement. He used that disagreement to slowly alienate me from my family and friends so all I had was him. I had no one to turn to when that first occurrence of physical abuse happened. I was in another city with no one but him. That is exactly what he wanted. Abusers alienate you from everyone. They don't want you to have anyone but themselves to turn to. They make you feel crazy for feeling the way you do when something isn't right. It's as if the abuser had a plan on how to break you down slowly from the start. How was I when I met him you probably are asking? I was always extremely confident and strong in who I was when I met him. I had everything. I changed slowly over time from the abuse. I was the girl in high school who said I would never be in an abusive relationship and that is exactly where I ended up. There were ups and downs. We did have some happy times and that is what keeps you holding on. They become glimmers of hope in the darkness. You believe their apologies over and over again because you want to believe things will change. It's never the abuser's fault. The abuser makes you believe you will never have better. They say things like who would want you and you will not leave me. Being in an abusive relationship is a form of brainwashing in some ways and you never see it coming. I kept thinking if I loved him enough, he should want to change for me and his child. People don't change because of anyone else; they have to see the issue and want to change.

Once my daughter was born it would be a while till, he was physically abusive to me again. I wasn't off the hook his emotional abuse became more intense. Emotional abuse is where it breaks you down to where there is nothing left in you. They manipulate you to believe that you would be nothing and do nothing without them. You doubt everything you once believed about yourself. To me, physical abuse is awful and can even be deadly. For me, emotional abuse was much worse only because physical abuse bruises go away over time. Emotional abuse goes so deep into your mental psyche. The emotional abuse tears you down and breaks you. It makes you question your self-worth. This abuse would go on throughout our relationship. Did we have good times you ask ever? We did and that was what you held on to. The false hope that it would get better. We eventually got married. We bought a beautiful brand-new home at the young age of 22 years old. I kept thinking that once we are married, buy a home and have a child that he should want to be better and he would be happy. I just kept thinking I could fix it. I felt all of those things would make everything better. What more could he want? It was always me trying to make it all right in his eyes and maybe I could help him. I wanted to give him all the things he didn't have growing up. I thought I could fill the voids of his childhood. I was so wrong. I would try for another child thinking this has to be it, the change needed. Mind you I loved being a mom that was one of my greatest joys and purposes in my life. I would miscarry twice not even seeing that maybe that was a sign of the stress I was under from our relationship. I would eventually get pregnant with my second greatest joy and blessing my second daughter. There honestly is no greater gift in this world than being a mom. They would have to watch my pregnancy closely. They were concerned due to my past history of miscarriages. Never once did I let on to doctors of my home life. She would end up being born and she was my second miracle baby.

At home, things were not always perfect but I was in love with my bundles of joy and with the thought of the family life I always wanted. I couldn't get divorced it was unseen in my family. I would be at home with our children making excuses why their daddy wasn't home. Once my kids fell asleep, I would call hospitals thinking he was involved in an accident or even worse dead somewhere. He always had excuses where he had been. He would say, "I stayed at a coworker's house we worked overtime. I was too tired to drive home. I went to see a friend and I just stayed there." They always seemed like valid excuses. He never would call to let me know he wouldn't be home. Of course, he did not like to be questioned. There would be times he would lash out and even throw things so you had to pick your battles. How do you not come home to your wife and your two daughters, especially one being a newborn? We have our beautiful daughters, our wonderful home, and great careers. What more could he want or need? It would be later confirmed that he had a drug and alcohol problem that he hid. There would be nights he wouldn't come home because he couldn't make it home. Happiness was short-lived. What I was hoping for was far from what it was.

At the time, I would be working from 7:30am to 6:00pm Monday through Friday. I would take my girls to work with me. My older daughter would be with me, my mom, or at preschool when she was old enough. My Dad once approached me and said, "don't you want to go home and spend time with him and the kids?" I threw myself into work because it was easier than dealing with the reality of what was happening at home. I was blessed to have the children with me always. I had that luxury since I was managing a business. I'd get home cook, clean, and get the kids ready at night and in the morning all by myself. It was rare I received help from him. I was getting severe migraines from the stress. I just blew it off as if I'm just tired. He became on edge more times than not. You felt like you were walking on eggshells constantly with him. One night he was mad about something small and he was being aggressive. There was no reasoning. I started planning a way to leave. I thought to myself I am raising my children on my own basically. Why am I staying for the little glimmer of hope and living a life of unhappiness? I had enough and it was time to go and take the girls with me. I packed up my car and left. He ended up following us and chasing us down the street with his car. I remember driving down streets trying to get away from him and thinking he will hurt us before he lets us go. He ended up yelling out the window ordering me, "Go home or else." I returned home terrified because I believed if I didn't, he would have caused an accident and not only hurt me but the girls. I once again was crying, scared and helpless. He would tell me that night, "You try to leave me and I'll find you, kill you and take the children." I felt there was no way out. There would finally be a night that would change it all for me and have me finally see the light at the end of the darkness. He became furious and I was trying to separate myself and the girls from his tirade. I ended up going upstairs to our bed with our younger daughter to avoid him and his rage. My older daughter was in her room next to ours. I always tried to protect my girls from seeing his anger as best as I could. I was laying there with my youngest daughter. She would have only been several months old. He shortly came in to our bedroom. He was upset that I wasn't listening to him. When he came in, I saw pure anger in his eyes that I had seen in the past. I was terrified not knowing what was next. He would never put his own daughter in danger. Would he? I knew right then it didn't matter to him. He leaned down and in his fit of rage would flip the mattress we were lying on. I knew we were going to go into the bassinet I had on the side of the bed. I put my arms around my baby protecting her and shielding her with my body and bracing for impact.

All I cared about at that moment was that she didn't get hurt. The sad thing was my older daughter was in the next room hearing it all. I at that moment stood up to him with my baby in my arms angry and said, "I will never let you hurt our children!" I was disgusted that he would harm his own child.

IT WAS TIME TO RISE

I made excuses for his actions and his reasoning for years. The moment he put our own children at risk I knew I had to leave for my own safety and theirs. I somehow convinced myself it was ok when it was me but never was going to be our children. This was not love. That night I was extremely upset and went to sleep in my four-year-old's room to separate ourselves from him. I so badly wanted my kids to have that family life I grew up in. I kept hoping if we loved him enough that it would make him want to change. Guess what? It wasn't and never would have been enough. The next thing my four-year-old daughter would say to me while her sister and I lay in her bed would save me and give me the power to leave. She was holding me as I was sobbing. She looked at me with such pure love and strength and told me, "One day we will get out of this." I will never forget that moment. I knew right then I had to do something to get us out. When your daughter at 4 years old says that it breaks your heart and you realize you think you're staying for them so they can have their family together. Even at her young age, she knew it was not right. She had more wisdom and strength at four than I had at 24 years old. I knew that night that I had to do something and plan how we were going to leave. Once he put our child at risk to that extent, I knew I had to leave for my safety and theirs. I could not let my children grow up thinking this was ok. I had to stop the cycle. It was time it ended here but I knew he wouldn't make it easy. I wanted so badly to give my girls the life I had growing up because they deserved that. My father was my everything. I so badly wanted that for them but I knew at that moment it would never be. I didn't see that our relationship was just hurting them. Those words my daughter spoke that night defined it for me. I can no longer raise my girls in this. I could not let them think this was normal. I had to show them strength. I would spend a couple of days depressed with my girls in my arms thinking how am I going to get out of this. That night he chased me down. When we got back to the house. He told me, "I will kill you before you ever take my kids from me." He also said," if you ever leave with them, I will hunt you down take them and kill you." That's all I could think of.

That night I realized I am dead if I stay. I finally found my way out. We would end up throwing a huge party for my youngest daughter's 1st birthday. It was a large party of around 75 people that were family and friends at my parents' house. He had promised to meet me there and his mom before the party started. Neither one ever showed up. I knew at that moment it was time to make my move. When a father doesn't show up for their daughter's birthday it tells you where their priorities are. It was always about him. Everyone at the party was asking me where the father was. No one knew the life I had been living for the last seven years behind closed doors. I always wanted to protect the ones I loved. I never wanted my parents or friends to know. You feel ashamed and weak for being in the situation you are in. The party ended and my mom would ask, "When are you going home?" That was the moment I knew I wasn't going home. I told her, "I am leaving him." That was my final breaking point and my way out. I was broken and I could no longer fight for something that wasn't worth fighting for. I had to for once put my girls and me first. I had to think about what was best for all of us. I no longer could have the guilt of what might happen to his health if I left. I could no longer worry about all of the what ifs. I finally choose my own happiness and my children's and we thrived because of it. I spent seven years of my life with him from 17 to 24 years old. I was young in love and wanted to believe in us. I've learned so much about myself through that journey. I learned what I did not want in my future. Staying in that relationship with him was killing the person I was and I no longer recognized the woman in the mirror. I am not the same person I was then. I'm stronger, wiser, happier, and determined to live a life I was always meant to have. I know my worth and love myself completely. I had some advice throughout those hard times that I will never forget. I was given advice and it always was in the back of my mind even if I didn't take action at the time.

In the end, the advice I was given throughout reminded me it was time to choose me finally. His mom would be one of those people along with my younger brother. His mom knew a little of what happened the day after I went to the hospital but never knew the full extent. She cried with me when I told her and she said, "You need to leave it's only going to get worse. I will always love you if that's what you choose. You will always be a daughter to me." She was right so early on. She gave me the ...it's ok to leave and think of you. I was in denial at the time. I also worried, what if something happened to him if I left. She would also share with me this explanation when I asked her when will I know if it's time to leave? "Your heart starts as a whole heart. As you go through hurtful times in your relationship whether it be from words or actions your heart will be affected. Those moments will break chips of your heart away until you have nothing left. When that happens, you will know when the time is right to leave." My younger brother who is one of my closest confidants who I knew would be honest, not judge, and is wise beyond his years would also give me clarity. We would meet and I would confide in him how I was unhappy in my marriage. He never knew the level of severity of my relationship. He only knew what I wanted him to know. I came to him so riddled with embarrassment and shame that I was even considering divorce. I grew up Catholic and it was considered a sin and we never had a divorce in my immediate family. I was having a hard time with it. He looked at me and said, "God doesn't want you to be unhappy. You have all of us that love you dearly. We will be here for you and the girls and anything you need. You will be ok and you are stronger than you think you are." He set me free and I felt this huge weight lifted off of me. I had to know and hear it was OK.

When I started dating my husband my heart was full and, in the end, there was nothing left. Years later my mom still not knowing what had happened in my past relationship with my daughters' dad would ask me a question. She would ask me, "Do you regret anything you went through with him?" I really do believe as a mom we sense things with our children. I immediately looked at her and with no hesitation, I said, "I regret not one thing." I learned so much and I have two of the most beautiful and precious girls a mother could ever ask for. I believe everything we go through happens for a reason. Our stories are what make us who we are. My daughters even with all that we went through were conceived with love. I look at them and I know one thing is for sure that they are the best part of both of us. That brings me peace. My daughters have turned into beautiful strong and outspoken women. I have brought them up and myself to know are worth and never let anyone treat you any less than you deserve. When I left, I realized how precious silence really was. I spent time with my girls reflecting on what I did and didn't want in my life. There was some healing to be had when I first left. I had to heal so I could show my daughters that we have so much strength within us. We can conquer anything we put our minds to.

We must listen to our heart but we must listen to what we know to be true. My why today are my girls. They are my everything in all that I do. I hear often people say I stay for my kids. Our children see, hear and sense everything. No matter how much you shield or protect them. I left when my girls were four and one years old and raised them as a single mom. I always wondered and thought my four-year-old was too young to remember anything. I left early enough I would tell myself. When she became 19 years old, I would finally ask her if she remembered anything. I was hoping she would say no. She would tell me she remembered everything. My heart broke at that moment when I heard those words. She looked at me and said, "But look how far you have come. I love you. I am proud of you and the woman you are." We often stay for the children but we need to ask ourselves is that the best for them.

The day I had my own place with my girls was one of the best days of my life. I sat there with them in silence emotional that we had nothing to fear any longer. I realized I might not have had what society tells you is the perfect family. Is there such a thing? Together my daughters and I were a family and they felt unconditional love. My daughters had an abundance of love from my family and friends. They grew up with my father and my brothers showing them love and what a man should be. I am grateful they had strong male figures in their lives. We often focus on everyone else's needs that we often put ours aside. We get so wrapped up in what society tells us is right or wrong. Who are any of us to judge? Loving oneself is the most powerful and rewarding gift you can give yourself. Our kids watch what we do. We must teach them it's OK to fall down but we must stand up and rise. It's rare I ever look back. In the rare instance, I do it's only to remind me how far I have come. We all have the past, present and future. What will you do with your past that can help you in your future? I have gratitude for my journey because it has led me here. Our stories are meant to be shared. We have no idea the impact we can make on someone's life by sharing our story. I hope if you or someone you know is going through something similar you know there is always a way out. I believe my journey was meant to be shared to hopefully empower the next person. We can only truly love someone else when we truly love ourselves first. Staying in a past situation only gives that power which no longer serves us. You deserve more. You deserve to have a life you desire to have. Always live your truth. I believe in you.

"If there is no peace in your past there is no power in your future." author unknown

I DECLARED MY INDEPENDENCE

Wow, how life has changed for all of us from where we were. I went on to vow to be the best version of myself in all capacities of my life for myself and my girls. I told myself I will never be weak again. That led me to join a gym and later compete in a figure competition. Lifting weights made me feel strong again. I know without a shadow of doubt that my girls were miracles put here on earth to teach me to be the woman I was always meant to be. I choose from that day forward to show them strength, unconditional love, and independence and to always believe in themselves. I taught them in a relationship that a person should add to your life not subtract from it. You are always good on your own and you don't need anyone. A relationship is a partnership a team effort. Someone in your life should enhance your life and together life is that much sweeter. I do believe God only gives us what we can handle. My girls will say that is one of my favorite sayings. They might be right. That saying helped me through many times. I do believe everything happens for reasons.

Life throws us moments whether good or bad that teaches us lessons. Sometimes those lessons do not come right away but the understanding will come over time. That day I left with my girls. I chose to be the victor and not the victim. I would years later buy a brand-new home on my own as a single mom. That moment was so empowering knowing I could do whatever I put my mind to and do it on my own. Leaving I claimed my independence emotionally and physically. Buying a home was independence on a financial level and all the possibilities that were still ahead. I can't even express the complete joy I had the day I received the keys to my new home with my young babies by my side. I was empowered. I went on to manage a few businesses to later own them and sell two of them. I am now a successful Realtor ® with my own real estate team. I have been awarded several awards from my office at Keller Williams for production. I also was honored to be the recipient of the Keller Williams Culture Award for 2020. I have graduated from our Keller Williams Bold Program multiple times. I was also asked this year to lead a team of 15 top realtors in that program. I am an investor and own my own rental properties. I also have a separate business managing commercial and residential properties for over 26 years.

I love empowering women whether it be in investing in real estate or teaching them what they are capable of. I find an abundant amount of joy teaching and empowering people to believe in themselves, their potential, their dreams, and their goals. I love what I do. I am extremely grateful to have the career I have. I was meant to be exactly where I am today. I am so proud of all I have accomplished and cannot wait for all that is ahead of me. I have two beautiful daughters who shine brighter than any star in this world. They are now 26 and 23 years old. My older daughter graduated college with multiple degrees. I always knew since the day she was born she would achieve amazing things in her lifetime. She was the first grandchild to attend a university and played lacrosse for the University of Arizona for a little over a year and a half to later transfer to the Fashion Institute of Fashion Design in Los Angeles. Fashion is definitely her calling. She is excelling in the fashion industry and her resume is extremely impressive at the young age of 26 years old. My youngest daughter is 23 years old and is my unbreakable warrior. She was diagnosed with Lyme disease and almost didn't make it a couple of times because of her health issues. She has come out stronger each time and always with a smile on her face no matter what she has been given. She is currently finishing her last year at a junior college and will be transferring to nursing to live her life's purpose. She wants to become a nurse because she knows how much a nurse can change the course of someone's health journey. She has a huge heart. I left when they were so young. I at times worried would they be ok? I second-guessed myself being a single mom. I just knew if I showed them love and gave them what I had growing up that they would be more than fine. We are so hard on ourselves as parents.

My girls often will tell me thank you for all that you were while we were growing up and the example you have set for us. We wouldn't have the life we have if it wasn't for you. I actually know I wouldn't have my life now if it wasn't for their constant support and love. I have always been honest with my girls throughout life. I always share all that I am and my different experiences in life. I wanted them to know no one is perfect and we all are learning along the way. I wanted them to learn through me. The relationship I have with my girls is beyond anything I could have ever imagined. We have the greatest mom and daughter relationships and we are the best of friends. There is nothing I wouldn't do for them. I often get told I hope I have the relationship you and your girls have. You all have the most fabulous relationship. They are the air I breathe and I thank God for them every day. They are my constant why day in and out. I want to not only leave them a legacy but live a legacy in all that I do. I am a strong and independent female who is grateful for the life I have been given. Every day I find gratitude in all that I am, the people that surround me, all that I have been blessed with, and especially my two daughters who always bring me so much joy, laughter and love. Storms will come in life but there is often a rainbow after the darkness to remind us of the beauty in all things. I am so proud of the women we have become and cannot wait to see what is in store for all of us as life goes on. I love the quote from Tony Robbins "Life happens for you not to you." I believe it to be true. I never once have looked at what I had to go through in a negative way because look where we all are now. We are women who are empowered, strong, successful, beautiful and intelligent, and ready to conquer. We know now, we can get through whatever life gives us and we will always become a better version of ourselves because of the experiences. We might believe our story has been written. Remember all you have to do to change the story is turn the page and write a new chapter in your story. Where will you lead yours?

ACKNOWLEDGEMENTS

To my best friends who are also my beautiful daughters. You two are the definition of strength, courage, compassion, joy, and love. Thank you for always being my biggest cheerleaders and pushing me to go beyond my comfort zone. Thank you for loving me the way you do. I am blessed for you two and am the woman I am today because of you both. We always will be the three musketeers. I love you both more than words could ever express. Love you every day!

To my parents thank you for teaching me to always believe in my dreams and to know anything is possible and never let anyone tell you differently. You both have taught me so much and I am grateful for the work ethic you have not only taught me but instilled in me. Thank you for teaching me and showing me and my daughters always unconditional love and always being there. Thank you for creating a beautiful family and legacy. Dad, you are no longer here but thank you for giving me the best father-daughter relationship that a girl could ever ask for. I strive to make you proud every day.

To the rest of my family thank you for loving me and being my biggest support system through it all. Michael thank you for always being there through all of my life adventures and simply being you. Love and appreciate you all!

Thank you to my friends, coaches, my tribe, and the powerhouse women who are in my life. Thank you for being who you all are and being part of my journey. I am beyond grateful to have you all in my life.

ABOUT THE AUTHOR

Giselle was born in Livermore, California. She is a mother to two phenomenal young women who amaze her every day. Giselle started managing businesses at 18 years old to own several companies' years later. She has her own property management business and has been in the industry for over 26 years. Giselle is an investor and owns her own rental properties. Her love and passion for real estate would lead her to receive her license as a REALTOR®. Giselle is the founder of the Giselle De Sousa Real Estate Team which has been serving clients for over 3 years. She is a multi-million-dollar selling REALTOR® and has received multiple awards from her brokerage, Keller Williams. Giselle's most current accolades are for her production in 2020 and the Keller Williams Culture Award for 2020. Her greatest joy is being a mother to her beautiful daughters who inspire her to be the woman she is today. Giselle believes we must not only leave a legacy but live a legacy in all we do every day. Giselle's ultimate goal is to empower, inspire and impact every person that crosses her path.

ABOUT MY BUSINESS

As the owner of both a Property Management Company for over 26 years and the founder of the Giselle De Sousa Real Estate Team for over 3 years. I am on a mission to empower everyone that crosses my path and inspire them. My goal is to educate and guide each person every step of the way on building their wealth through real estate while exceeding their expectations. It is true happiness when I am able to hand clients keys to their new home, selling a client's home as they move on to new adventures and/or helping them buy investment properties. My clients truly are friends that become family. I love what I do and am blessed to help so many incredible people.

Facebook Personal Page
Giselle De Sousa

Facebook Business Page
SoldbyGiselle

Instagram Personal
Giselle.yourrealtor

Instagram Business
SoldbyGiselle

Website:
GiselleDeSousa.com

THANK YOU!

I hope you found yourself inspired. If you found yourself in the story, I want you to choose you! We are all powerful, unbreakable and unstoppable. If you know someone in a similar situation please share my story to encourage and empower them. Our stories are meant to be shared thank you for letting me share mine. Feel free to connect with me or follow me on my social media platforms for inspiration, all things real estate, my adventures, and of course my family.

ACKNOWLEDGMENTS

It takes a village to produce a book, and I am deeply grateful for the creative forces and dedication of every single person who added her or his magic to this one.

This is the seventh book in our Don't Be Invisible Be Fabulous series – and I am deeply honored.

My whole-hearted appreciation starts with the readers and supporters of our first, best-selling book; they inspired the second, third, fourth, fifth, sixth and now seventh volume. This journey reinforced in my bones how essential it is to tell stories of real-life women triumphing in their lives. Thousands of women saw themselves in those stories, and then they could imagine a way forward in their own lives. So, of course, Volume 7, featuring more stories of hope and inspiration, had to be born!

Heaps of appreciation also go to the fabulous coauthors from our first, second, third, fourth, fifth and sixth books:

Thank you all!

The Entrance To The World Of Aligning To A More Fabulous You.

Working with women on visibility is a love of mine. Because once upon a time, I hid. Once upon a time, I was a Corporate Good Girl.

RESOURCES

Programs

VOICE and VISIBLITY Virtual Group Coaching program: 90 days of transformational coaching experience. You have the right to take up space on this planet and be seen and heard. As you. The real you. Cuz no one– not anyone– can compete with the real, true. You.

This program is here so you can bring your badass out.... and create the movement, money, and message your meant to blaze in the world.

I am so passionate about being a catalyst that mentors visionary women like you to to claim your voice in a clear way, so you create visibility and wealth...

Wanna make your voice heard?
This work starts when you say yes.
Message me now to talk, to see, and to know.

Message me on FB Messenger to inquire about coaching or sharing your story in our next book.
@m.me/dorrisburch

Free Resources

Podcast:
New Fab You Show with the fabulous Dorris Burch

This is a podcast for the woman who no longer desires to Whisper. Hide. Doubt. Shut down…

You know I'm so about visibility and full self-expression so you can STAND OUT in your biz and life.

Don't miss an episode: NewFabYouShowPodcast.com
Subscribe and leave a review

Become A Fab Factor Brand Ambassador

If you believe that…

There is **Power** in the **Voice** in a Fabulous Woman… There is **Purpose** in the **Life** of a Fabulous Woman… There is **Passion** in the **Heart** of a Fabulous Woman…

Get your No Cost image at… BeFabulousImage.com

SOCIAL MEDIA

Website
TheFabFactor.com

Facebook Page
https://www.facebook.com/thefabfactoracademy

Instagram
@IAmTheFabulousDorrisBurch

YouTube
https://www.youtube.com/c/dorrisburch

ABOUT THE FABULOUS DORRIS BURCH

THE FABULOUS DORRIS BURCH is a world-renowned thought shaker for women Up-Leveling their Visibility. To get noticed in your message + movement just by being fully YOU. Through her "New Fab You Show" podcast, virtual group program and mastermind for high-level visionary women entrepreneurs, and compiler of the bestselling "Don't Be Invisible Be Fabulous" anthology book series, and her bestselling "The Little Black Book Of

Being Fabulous" book, and her daily free inspirational posts, and videos distributed across her social media channels, for over a decade she has been helping women to step into the most powerful versions of themselves to be fabulous and design lives and businesses they are wildly obsessed with to create their most fabulous lives. Her mission is for women globally to Don't Be Invisible. Be Fabulous!

Combining a background in fashion merchandising as well as human resources and metaphysical science with practical business advice and a deep knowledge of spiritual and energetic principles, Fabulous Dorris isn't quite like any other "coach" you've encountered. A true self-made fabulous woman. She credits her success to her sheer determination, a deep desire to serve others, and an unwavering belief in her own dreams to be seen and heard in a big way.

Fabulous Dorris has earned a master of public affairs in government/business relations, a master of arts in human resources & management and a bachelor of science in fashion merchandising and a bachelor's in metaphysical science. She is currently completing her doctorate in metaphysical science. In addition to many many certifications in coaching and leadership.

She is a native of Kansas City, Missouri, but currently lives in the Chicagoland area with her husband and son.

Made in the USA
Monee, IL
23 December 2021

f187d159-8678-46e5-9ca4-8760713609caR01